FROM THE EAGLE'S WING

FROM THE EAGLE'S WING

a biography of JOHN MUIR

HILDEGARDE HOYT SWIFT

illustrated by LYND WARD

WILLIAM MORROW and COMPANY
New York   1962

DEDICATION

To all lovers of the wilderness,
Our most priceless American possession,
And to their children's children,
Who will save and protect it,
This book is dedicated.

*"Probably the truest lover of Nature,
as she appears in woods, mountains, glaciers,
we have ever had."*

John Burroughs

Foreword

IT HAS BEEN A GREAT PLEASURE AND PRIVILEGE FOR ME TO
have the opportunity to read the biography of John Muir
by Hildegarde Hoyt Swift. This is the life of a man who
must have been a most fascinating human being, but what
he has accomplished in his life is of value to every one of
us today. He really started the concept of conservation,
which I think needs to be revived, and I hope that this
book *From the Eagle's Wing*, which to me was so fascinating that I could hardly put it down, will give the people
of this country who read it a sense of the urgency which
we should have about preserving our heritage of woods
and soil and wilderness. We must have the trees to keep
our water table high and to break the winds, so that our
topsoil is not carried away either by flood or wind. We
must have the wilderness to preserve the animals and the
beauties that can be so easily destroyed by man but can
never be brought back.

I am happy to have had a chance to write this short
foreword and to congratulate the author on having

brought this man alive in a way which makes us feel his vitality, his charm, and his dedication.

This book is a service to the memory of a great human being and at the same time to the country that he loved, which must not become a destroyer of its own beauties and its own natural resources.

ELEANOR ROOSEVELT

April 13, 1961

Introduction

I SHOULD LIKE TO SAY THAT THIS BIOGRAPHY OF JOHN
Muir, like my earlier life of John Burroughs, "The Edge
of April," is dramatized, not fictionized. Rather, it is
based on long and careful study in various libraries, on
facts and incidents and descriptions taken from Muir's
own books and journals. Some of the latter I have read
in the original, little rain-soaked diaries, written by a
lonely campfire, or with numbed fingers on some mountain glacier.

My book is also based on personal letters, such as the
unpublished Pelton correspondence at the University of
Wisconsin, or the correspondence with Robert Underwood Johnson of the *Century Magazine* at the Bancroft
Library of the University of California, or the privately
printed letters to Mrs. Ezra Carr, which I found at Yale.

I am grateful for many intangibles, gained from talking with individuals who "knew John Muir when . . ."
Some of these people were children when they knew
him, but they remember. Above all, I am indebted to

Mrs. Helen Muir, devoted younger daughter of John Muir, who still keeps her father's name. She has given me much information and shared with me invaluable insights.

I have called my book "From the Eagle's Wing" not only because Muir's earlier articles were written with an eagle's quill, but also because the eagle always seems to be his fitting counterpart. When Emerson visited the Yosemite, Muir said to him, "You are yourself a sequoia —stay and get acquainted with your great brothers!" In much the same way, I say the eagle is John Muir's symbol. He could fly higher, on more powerful wings of the imagination than the run of men. Like the eagle, he was at home on lonely heights or in dark, mysterious forests. He was strong, daring, and free, master of wind and space, man-eagle or eagle-man.

If I have managed to capture in this narrative even a fraction of the passionate zest for life, the love of beauty, or the dedication to his own sense of mission which characterized John Muir, I shall be more than content.

HILDEGARDE H. SWIFT

Rhinebeck, New York
January 18, 1961

Contents

FROM THE EAGLE'S WING

1

The Daring
Scootchers

THE LITTLE SCOTCH TOWN OF DUNBAR STOOD DOURLY IN
its ring of hills, facing the North Sea. Crooked, cobble-
stoned streets wound down to the harbor and beaches at
its foot, and the reddish-gray stones of the tall, unadorned
houses, the purple slates of their roofs, glistened with the
salt wet which the sea wind brought to them. Forever the
wind swept through the winding streets carrying the leaves
of fall scurrying before it or lifting the dust of summer. In
winter it bore the scud and spindrift of the great storms
high up the land into entryways and walled gardens,
drenching the nearby houses till they stood swept and
clean.

For a thousand years, since the days of the Picts and
Romans, old Dunbar Castle had towered on the headland
beside the harbor, dark and grim like some giant cormo-
rant with outstretched wings. Now its walls were crumbling and the waves had eaten their way even into the
dungeons at its base.

To small John Muir, son of Ann and Daniel Muir, born

15

on the twenty-first of April, 1838, the seaport town of
Dunbar was the best possible place in which to grow up.
From the first he was a strong and lively little boy with
the look of the Celt plain upon him, the bright blue eyes
and vivid copper-colored hair of the true Gael. His home
was a wonderful place, large and comfortable, where the
sternness of Father, the gentleness of Mother, the lax dis-
cipline of servants, and the friendly rivalry of older sisters
all combined to give him room to grow.

Across the street was the most fascinating playmate
of all—Grandfather Gilrye, his first teacher and friend.
John had hardly learned to walk when he began to scram-
ble after him, firmly clinging to the gnarled old hand and
puffing like a worried little terrier.

One morning when Johnny Muir was two years old
he was waked up early by a firm hand on his shoulder.
At once he squirmed away from it, then opened his eyes
to find his father's face, dim in the half-light, bending
over him. At first he was startled and a bit anxious, till
he saw that the usually stern face was smiling.

"Run to your mither's room and see what's come," his
father told him.

Like a small whirlwind Johnny was out of bed, trot-
ting on fat legs down the hall. Something nice? A present
for him?

Mother was still asleep in the wide four-poster; at least
her eyes were closed. But she opened them to smile down
at the solemn little boy, waiting eagerly there for her
attention. Then she pulled down the thick comforter

from a tiny, red-faced, squirming little thing in the bed beside her.

"See, Johnny, your wee, bonnie new brother!"

"Bonnie?" This ugly, twisting bundle that was making thin, squawky noises, not as sleek as a kitty or cuddly as a puppy. Not bonnie at all—and certainly no present for him. He put out a quick hand and poked at the bundle hard, where the most squirm seemed to be.

"He's no good!" he said, his lower lip trembling.

But time went by and the ugly squirming thing turned into a jolly, mischievous small boy who followed his older brother like a shadow. Davie was fun; Davie liked to dig in the sand and play in the pools on the rocks; Davie liked to hide in the garden. Soon John began to feel a fiercely protective love for the little brother with his bright eyes and brown hair.

Johnny was not yet four when his father called him one night and said, "Tomorrow, son, ye'll go to the Davel Brae School. The Devil finds work for idle hands to do. From now on ye'll play no more."

Johnny looked firmly back into his father's stern blue eyes, so like his own in shape and color, and blinked manfully to keep away the tears. He wasn't ready yet to think of school.

But the next day when Maggie scrubbed his face till it shone, and helped him into his red flannel petticoat and bright kilt of the Gordon tartan, he settled down to the sticky Scotch oatmeal porridge in his wooden luggie with a right goodwill. Then Mother kissed him and, slipping a primer into a small green bag, hung the strap of it about his neck. Sister Sarah took him firmly by the hand till, breaking away from her, he scampered on quite proudly by himself.

"To the Davel Brae, the Davel Brae," he chanted, as the green bag streamed behind him in the wind and his Glengarry cap twisted down over one ear.

Mungo Siddons, the dominie teacher, was tall, black-clad, and terrifying. The sight of the ready leather tawse leaning against his chair on the platform did not make him less so. Only his bright red nose, in such strange contrast to his dark, glowering look, suddenly made him seem funny and human.

"Johnny Muir, do you know your letters?"

John swallowed over a very large lump in his throat, looked straight back at the old man, and answered, "Aye, sir."

"Come here, John!"

Yielding but little, John took one step forward. It was then that a transforming smile broke over the lined, brown face; one hand dipped under the black coat and came out closed. The next minute John's two hands were full of gooseberries.

That first morning at school was dull, tiresome, and endless. Wedged between two older boys, close to the front and under the eyes of the teacher, there was nothing to do but sit still—or try to. The boys didn't help. One of them kicked John savagely on the calf, and the boy on the other side pinched him, all by way of welcome to the Davel Brae. But Johnny ignored the pinch and returned the kick with interest—one good hard sideways whack, effective because unexpected. The boy yelped and old Mungo, raising his leather whip, shook it in the air a moment by way of warning.

Endless! John's stout legs prickled; his whole body quivered with restlessness. At the first clang of the recess bell he was up, jumping the bench in front of him. But alas for his haste, from somewhere in the inner depths there came a ripping sound; a button popped; the bright red petticoat slid down around his feet. Grandly ignoring it, he dashed for liberty.

But the return from recess brought the bitter climax. There stood Mungo on the platform, waving the red skirt like a flag. "Who owns this? Who owns this pettiskirt?" he roared.

Not for worlds would Johnny have answered. But one of the older girls cried, "Johnny dropped it—wee Johnny Muir. I saw him." So John marched forward to claim his own, his first solo appearance in school to the tune of snickers and catcalls.

When the school closed and he stood waiting in the yard for Sarah to come from the grammar school, a howling pack of small savages rushed by, taunting him. "Girlie, girlie, dropped your petticoat, yah!" The boys yelled while the girls made faces.

But it was not long before Johnny Muir found his rightful place in the Davel Brae School, never to lose it again. Not many months before the tune changed. The boys began to call him a good fighter and "Dux" of the little boys. The girls chose him first in their games.

There was one thing above all others that Johnny loved and that was the coming of a gale. He loved to hear the roar of the great breakers as they tore up the beach to break in stinging fury on the rocks. Excitement—thrilling and terrible! In some curious way he responded with joy to the wildness of the storm. Best of all he liked to see the white spray dash itself mountains high against the ruined walls of Dunbar Castle, till spray and wind and driving rain all seemed part of some great drama, played by giants to a mysterious end.

After such storms the beach was littered with objects, often from some pitiful wreck. Casks and boxes and broken spars—there was no telling what treasure might wash up at one's feet. At times like these, men, women, and ragged children haunted the sands, looking for loot. Once John saw the surface of the waves covered with small, round things like red birds with folded wings. When he found they were apples, he waded into the water to grab his share.

As the months lengthened and the years grew, John and Davie were in and out of mischief as regularly as the tides rose on the shore. John was always the leader, by virtue of his extra two years and his own right as well. For he was strong, sturdy, and restless, always looking for a new game or a new "scootcher," as he called the tests of courage that he invented. Davie followed his

brother in all the "awfu' scootchers," though it sometimes took more courage than he had.

All Scottish children grow up on tales of ghosts, witches, and boo-wuzzies, their sure legacy in the land of mist, along with stories of ancient battles, old wrongs to be righted, and wonderful derring-do. Was there a ghost in their own house? "Aye," John whispered to Davie, "the ghost of the old doctor. I'll just go and give myself a bit o' a fright!"

"Oh, don't, John—don't! Tarry a blink!" Davie begged piteously. But Johnny was off, his bare feet pattering down the hall in the half-darkness, on into the room that was always kept closed with stern warnings to stay out on peril of an "awfu' whipping." It had belonged to a doctor who once owned the house in which the Muirs now lived and his tall glass tubes, beakers, and retorts still stayed in the place where he had mixed his mysterious potions.

Slowly, slowly, Johnny pushed open the creaking door. There were the dusty little windows, lit with a dim moonlight, one small ray of which caught the glass of a test tube, lighting it for a moment with a spectral gleam. Hush! Was that something moving there in the shadows? Trembling with delicious terror, Johnny turned and shot from the room.

Poor Davie! Now it was his turn to take the dreadful journey.

"It's not so far away, Davie!" Johnny encouraged him.

"It's an awfu' good scootcher. Don't cry, Davie!"

If this was a good scootcher, John soon thought of another one that held a different kind of fright equally thrilling. Two nights later, when the moon was at its full, he climbed up to the high dormer window which looked from his bedroom out over the back garden. No, nobody would see him!

He doubled up and climbed out the little window carefully. The night wind ballooned his nightshirt and sent it billowing about him; the coolness of the wind soothed his small, bare body. He held on the sill hard and hung himself out into space, with a wary eye for the roof slates below him. Then he dared Davie to try it too.

But this was not enough. Standing on the sill by the left wall of the window, he managed to creep up the slates till he reached the roof of the dormer. There he sat proudly astride, while the wind mocked him and the noise of it was loud in his ears. Then he slipped back the way he had come and, catching the sill, was soon in his room again.

Davie, too, climbed up to the dormer roof, thrusting his spindly legs bravely across it. But here the sight of the garden far, far below filled him with dizziness and terror.

"I can't get down! Oh, I can't get down!" he wailed, till Johnny answered firmly, "Stop crying, Davie! Father will hear and give us both an awfu' whipping. Put your feet in my hands!"

Standing on the sill, he caught his little brother's heels,

jumped inside and dragged Davie after him. There was no doubt that this was an "awfu' good scootcher."

When Johnny Muir had just turned seven and started on toward eight, he left the Davel Brae School and his small brother, Davie, behind him. Left, too, the kindly care of Mungo Siddons, who, though he brandished the strap, also handed out gooseberries and currants and gave the boys many little vacations when he went outside for "a wee drap o' the usual."

Dominie Lyon of the grammar school was made of sterner stuff. The tawse in his hands left a serious mark. Serious, too, and not to be taken lightly were the tasks which he set. Every day there were lessons to be learned in Latin, French, and English, grammar to be committed to memory and recited, just as if the horrible rules and verbs were poetry. Besides that, there were spelling, history, arithmetic, and geography. John never knew when next he would be pounced upon.

"John Muir, rise and conjugate the Latin verb *to be!*" the master demanded, and John, bowing, began hopefully, "Sum, es, est . . . sumus . . ." But soon there came a slip, a great, yawning, terrifying gap in his memory, and now the strap, stinging and cutting across his hands.

Big boys "didn't cry" either inside the school or out on the playground, and the sturdy son of the Muir family early learned to toss back his copper-colored hair, square his shoulders, and clamp his lips together in a firm, thin line. He'd be a true Muir of the Gordon clan, a High-

lander who fought with Wallace and raised the great
Bruce to Kingship. The boy early learned to take his
whippings in silence.

New to the school, he had to take his medicine out
on the playground too, meeting one by one the boys who
challenged him.

"What are ye glowerin' at, John?"

"I'll look where I have a mind! Stop me if you dare!"

"I'll let you see whether I dare or no!"

From then on the battle was joined, sometimes to be
settled at once, sometimes to be carried to the seashore
and finished after school. If John carried home the true
marks of conflict—bleeding lip and black eye—Mother had
to rush him to bed before Father came back from the
store. For Father always thrashed him for fighting.

Of all his studies geography was the one which seemed
to have most meaning. Other parts of the world, especially wonderful, wild America, he carried happily in his
mind and heart. He would go to visit them, someday.
The playground back of the school ran up at the end
into a rise of ground from which he could see the ocean.
Here he often stood, watching the careening ships—brigs,
schooners, or great square-riggers, their sails white against
the blue or dim in mist and spume against the gray. To
what far ports were they sailing?

Sometimes, too, John could see far out, almost lost in
the distance, a covey of ships waiting the turn of the
tide to carry them up the Firth to Edinburgh. It was all
wonderful. His thoughts seemed to fly away on the wind.

He always loved the smell of salt and the slap of waves against the playground wall. In these days, too, he began to whittle toy boats to play with, and all his schoolbooks were edged with drawings of sailing ships.

When he was nine, John, Willie Chisholm, Bob Richardson, and several other fellows belonged to a gang which ranged the countryside far and wide in search of adventure. Davie, too, was a tag-along, whenever he could run away. Sometimes they tore along the roads for hours, tiring each other out in races, or, choosing leaders and sides, re-enacted the battles of long ago. Shouting the old battle cries, "Bannockburn, Bannockburn, Scotland forever!" they stuffed their Scotch blue bonnets with sand or gravel and turned them into vicious weapons.

Sometimes, exhausted, they lay on their backs, watching the larks hovering over the meadows, singing and soaring, rising higher and higher, bursting into glorious music until they were lost to view, one with the clouds and the sky. It was a test of eyesight to be able to follow the larks into space.

"I see mine—mine yet!" John cried.

"Mine's there. I see mine!" Bob answered, until one of them triumphed in the contest.

Sometimes they climbed trees to peer into nests or swing from branches or try for the greatest height. Sometimes they broke through hedges, scaled garden walls, stole apples and pears, wild as young hawks enjoying their wildness. Passing farmers brandished their whips and shouted, "Back to th' town wi' ye, you villains!" But little the boys cared. Hooray for the next adventure! Back to town? Not till dark was settling down!

On weekdays John had no time for such mad-rabbiting. School kept him late. But when Saturday arrived, all the repressed energies of the week were looking for an outlet. In vain Father tried to shut John and Davie into their own back garden, with threats of an "awfu' thrashing" if they ran again with that pack of vagabonds. But the boys early learned to scale a wall by standing one on the other's shoulders. John climbed up on Davie, reached for the top, pulled up his brother, then lowered him on the other side. What if the gate was locked? No locks or threats of thrashings could stop them.

It was spring and the boys had found a lark's nest set in the long grass of their favorite meadow west of Dunbar. As usual, John saw it first and stood claiming it, holding off all comers. Inside, the young birds were just ready to fly. That night, when the lads turned toward home, there was a young lark beating and fluttering its wings inside John's jacket.

Mother looked aghast when she saw what he had brought.

"He'll make me a fine pet," John cried defensively. "I'll feed him a' he needs!"

For a long while Mother withheld her answer. Then she said, "Bring down th' old empty linnet cage from the attic, John."

For many days John was devotion itself to the small prisoner that lived in its cage at the south window. Water, all the insects he could catch, a nice, fresh stretch of sod across the floor of its prison. But the little hostage from the wild pined and was far from happy.

Early one lovely Saturday, when the rare sunshine flooded the world, John carried the cage outside and hung it from a drooping tree branch. Then he saw a strange thing. As if waked from a long sleep by the sudden warmth, or by some special message from the outdoor world, the young lark chirped and called, spread its wings and, hopping to the top of its cage, tried to hover there, as all its lark kind had hovered for hundreds of years over the wild meadows.

Something in John's heart seemed to yield. A hard wall of selfishness broke in pity and remorse. Without a word to anyone, he seized the cage, went through the garden gate, and trudged the long miles back to the west meadow where he had found the nest. Here he set his fledgling free, feeling a strange rush of joy and exaltation when— a streak of brown and gold—the wild thing flew away.

If John and his friends liked to chase over the roads, meadows, and farms of the inland country, even more they loved the wild, irregular shore. Most exciting of all were the days when they explored Dunbar Castle, grim and crumbling on its high, rocky point by the sea.

Because of the wonderful scootchers which they found there, the boys loved to climb the walls and explore the deep dungeons below. Once these had never seen the light of day, but now the sea had battered and eaten its way into the very heart of them. That, too, made the dark, crumbling stone rooms tricky and dangerous to enter, for one must keep a wary eye out for the turn of the tide.

One day Willie, Bob, John, and Davie crept along the mouldering wall to a point where they could look down into the deepest pit of all.

"Och!" said John. "It's awfu' dark and deep."

"You daren't go down," cried Bob with a snicker. "You daren't!"

"Bosh!" said John. " 'Tis scary—but I'll go!"

"Oh, don't, Johnny, don't go down," begged Davie.

Soon, like a mountain goat, John was inching his way down the steep wall, feeling with foot and hand for the projecting rocks, testing them carefully, then moving slowly on. The light grew dimmer; the air of the dungeon was heavy with damp and rank with decay, the rocks slippery with wet and slime. It was hard to hold them firmly; it was hard to keep his feet from sliding. If both hands and feet should fumble—what then?

Even as he thought it, his right foot lost its precarious place, and the rock beneath his left one broke, letting him swing free. Still clinging, he felt his hands grow numb and weak, lose their hold until, struggling and clutching, slowly, then faster and faster, his helpless body slid down into space.

The water into which he fell seized his ankles with an icy clutch. Now his knees. Now it seemed to suck him down, down. At first he plunged and floundered wildly; then, remembering the pools where he often played and the waves through which he loved to dive, confidence returned to him. Letting his body relax in the water, he found that it only reached to his shoulders and that his feet could touch solid ground.

When John came to the top of the wall again, his face and hands were streaked with dirt and blood, his clothes torn to shreds and dripping with slimy water, but he smiled a triumphant smile, calmly ignoring Davie's excitement and the other fellows' praise.

Not long after this greatest and hardest of all his scootchers, Maggie scolded him for saying the evil words, "Devil take it!"

"You'll go to Hell, Master John, 'deed, that you will, if you keep on."

"An I do go down to Hell," John answered firmly, "I'll just climb out again! I know I can. I have done it a'ready."

If there was one word which stood for the most important thing John learned in the winter of '48, it was the word *America*. In school, dry old Dominie Lyons seemed to come alive with a new enthusiasm. He told them of valleys full of gold just found in California, of how men were sailing from far ports of call to try their luck in the gold rush.

More exciting to John than the gold, the master gave his school pages of natural history to learn, filled with stories of the beautiful, unspoiled wilderness across the sea; tales of Indians, eagles, and fishhawks, tales of passenger pigeons, of maple trees that ran rivers of sweetness in spring.

"And who was the man who came to Scotland but a few years since with pictures of American birds?"

"Audubon," cried Johnny without a moment's hesitation.

"Right, John Muir! You may turn to page twenty-five of Maccoulough and read us the description there in Audubon's own words."

Yes, Johnny knew his Audubon and was thrilled by his vivid account of the New World, though he grew angry each time he read again how the beautiful passenger pigeons were ruthlessly slaughtered. Word after word—he knew it all by heart.

"This is the wonderful story of the passenger pigeon, a beautiful bird flying in vast flocks that darkened the sky like clouds, countless millions assembling to rest and sleep and rear their young in certain forests, miles in length and breadth, fifty or a hundred nests on a single tree. . . .

"Not a pigeon had arrived at sundown. Suddenly a cry arose, 'Here they come!' The noise they made reminded me of a hard gale at sea, passing through the rigging of a close-reefed ship. Thousands were soon knocked down by the pole men. The birds continued to pour in. . . . It was a scene of uproar and conflict. I found it useless to speak, or even to shout to those persons nearest me.

. . . I was aware of the firing only by seeing the shooters reloading. . . .

"Then the authors of all this devastation began their entry amongst the dead, the dying, and the mangled. The pigeons were picked up and piled in heaps."

Yes, Johnny knew his Audubon. He read the vivid story over and over, in spite of the heartbreak it brought him.

If school was different and exciting that winter when John was ten, home, too, seemed to be changing in mysterious ways. There was an undercurrent of tension running through the house, which Johnny felt, but did not understand. Over and over, it seemed, Mother and Father were having long talks together, but when John came by and stood for a moment to listen, suddenly the talk was of school or of little Annie's last attack of croup.

Below stairs there was a clatter and chatter such as Johnny had never heard before. But when he asked Maggie, "What's all the clishmaclaver?" she tossed her head and answered, "Don't you know, Master John, you're goin' . . ." and then she clapped a fat, red hand over her mouth, looked scared, and would say no more.

Christmas and New Year's came and went; already it was middle February with a hint of spring, and the first signs of snowdrops in the back garden. Soon he would be loafing along the shore, watching the purple dulses swaying in all the pools, picking up crabs and starfish, plunging into the surf.

Then came the night when John and Davie were sitting by Grandfather Gilrye's fire just across the street, trying to write their Latin compositions, bothering the old man for help with a word or two. Suddenly the front door banged and Father was in the room, waving his arms and shouting. Very strange, this, for he rarely came here! He and Grandpa had had some ancient feud and there was no love lost between them.

"Bairns, bairns," Father shouted, tense with an excitement they had never seen in him before, "you need not learn your lessons th' night for we're going to America the morn! Awa' wi' you to your mither," he added, and disappeared.

A few moments longer the boys lingered, wild with excitement themselves, pouring out an incoherent chatter of gold and trees full of sugar just for the taking. "And no more school!" chanted Davie, doing a little private jig to celebrate.

"Poor laddies!" Grandpa said slowly and sadly. "You'll find something else over the sea but gold and sugar, birds' nests and freedom from lessons and schools. You'll find plenty hard, hard work." How often later they were to remember Grandfather Gilrye's words.

The old man turned to a cupboard set high up in the paneled wall above the fireplace, pulling out a small brown box with cautious hands; an ancient carved box, which had a wonderful jingle as it moved. Out of the depths of it Grandpa fished two gold coins, handing them solemnly to his grandsons. Brilliantly they flashed in the firelight before two grubby fists swallowed them up. "For good-by!" Grandpa said.

Cold winter fog stood thick in the High Street next morning when the little group found their way to the railroad station. When John learned that only he and Sarah and Davie were going with Father, all his first excitement changed to fear. To leave Mother—that he could hardly bear. But Mother smiled at him as she gave him the news, softening it with the sure promise that she and Margaret, the oldest, would be "coming over soon," when Father had found "just the house for the wee bairns." With that John had to be content. As the train pulled away and, with face pressed close to the window, he saw his mother disappear, he put out his hand to Sarah and caught hold of her desperately. She had always been a kind of foster mother to him. Perhaps the fourteen-year-old girl was none too sure of herself, but she held John's hand tight in her own and squeezed it hard.

At the Glasgow dock, the sailing ship that would be their home for many weeks lay rocking gently with the tide. Quickly John swarmed up the gangplank, yanking Davie along behind him. Soon the two boys were scampering about from stern to bowsprit, staring up at the high poop, inspecting the rigging, watching the sailors handling the snaking ropes, peering down into the deep, dark hold. About them people of all ages and from many nations milled and chattered.

At the turn of the tide all visitors were sent ashore,

the gangplank was lifted aboard, the ship threw off her hawsers and, with foresail raised, slid slowly out into the main current. Now the forest of masts stood behind them; the gulls dipped and screamed about them; the docks and buildings of Glasgow, the tall spires and bridges, grew dim and distant; the banks of the Clyde slid slowly by like something in a dream.

As the sunset light stood in the west, the sails were hoisted, even to the last topgallant and the wind filled them, turning them into luminous wings. John's eyes followed the mainmast up, up to the sky. Above it he caught the sharp prick of a new star. The good salt of the open sea filled his nostrils and he thrilled to the sudden tilt of the deck, as the ship quivered, then plunged faster across the waves.

In the half-light, John saw the immensity of the ocean about him, the vast, mysterious water without beginning and without end. All his life he had been a child of the sea, living on the edge of it, watching its moods and changes. Well he knew its cruelty and power. How often he had picked up on the beach bits of broken spars and other tokens of shipwreck! How often he had heard tales of "another ship foundered and all hands lost!"

As he stood watching, a terrible solemnity rolled over and engulfed the excitement of a moment before. This thin wall of wood was all that stood between him and the awful mystery beneath. Cold and growing darkness and the bitter February wind.

But as he threw back his head and squared his shoulders and felt the salt spray in his face, a thrilling sense of joy returned. All the excitement of uncertainty and a passionate love of it. This was better than the hardest scootcher. John Muir was starting his first real adventure.

With wind east-nor'-east and all sails set, the schooner sped westward into the open ocean.

2

"Splash into Pure Wildness"

SATURDAY, NOVEMBER 7TH, WAS A CLEAR, BRIGHT DAY IN the Wisconsin country. No snow on the good, firm earth. All day the three children watched the edge of the woods, where a stretch of new corduroy led to the farm. But now it was getting late.

Sarah was anxious, John could see, though she sat quietly, back against a tree trunk, hands folded. Davie was trying his cart wheels, now with legs high in air, now hitting the earth with a thump.

"Why doesn't Mother come?" he asked, as he turned right side up. "Maybe something's happened!"

"Whisht!" said Sarah roughly—rough, John knew, because she cared so much.

"Such a long way," John said thoughtfully. "First the ocean, then the Hudson River and the Erie Canal."

"Injun country," Davie interrupted. "Just the way we came!"

"Yes. Then the Great Lakes, Milwaukee—a long ride

through the wilderness—how can we expect her to be on time?"

"But Father wrote t'would be today."

It was John who saw the first distant motion—leaves waving at the edge of the forest, white heads of Tom and Jerry, the oxen, poking through, the sledge with its precious cargo. With a whoop of joy he started down the slope.

"Mother's here!"

Ann Muir climbed down over the edge of the sledge, shaking out her skirts, pushing the black bonnet back from her broad, gentle face.

"Bairns, bairns!" she cried, holding out her arms.

"My own lassie," she whispered, as Sarah clung to her, all the loneliness of many weeks set free in a burst of tears. Half shyly, John seized her hand and she raised her other one, pushing the straggling locks back from his forehead, looking questioningly into his brilliant blue eyes. "A brave, big laddie you've come to be, Johnny!" Young Daniel capered about, the twins shrieked with glee, chasing Watch, the pup; and Margaret kissed them all. Father Daniel for once smiled broadly at each one of them. It was a fine, proud home-coming.

First of all Mother must be shown the new house. They trooped after her, as she climbed the front steps, but waited for her to go ahead of them. "Home at last!" she said happily, as she pushed open the heavy door. For a moment she stood on the threshold; now quietly, as if in a dream, she moved on from room to room—looking, looking.

"Well, lassie, is it not bonnie?" Father Muir cried, impatient for praise. She turned to him warmly, reaching out to seize his arm.

" 'Tis bonnie indeed, Daniel—every room bonnie. To build a house like this—'tis a wonder altogether!" And Father Muir fairly glowed with pride.

Like a gay army, they marched along with Mother, showing her everything inside and outside the house; the newly roughed out flower beds in front, now stiff with frost, which John and his father had made ready for her seeds; the way to the lake, down through its lovely, spring-fed meadow; the queer mounds at the other side. "Injun graves," Davie told her cheerfully.

Then the upper field, which Father and the Yankee who worked for them had cleared, the shanty in which they had first lived. Best of all, John proudly showed her Jock, the beautiful roan with the long, sweeping black tail, his own horse which Father had bought from an Injun and given just to him.

"Understands Scotch," he boasted to his mother, "though he never heard anything but Winnebago before!"

December brought bitter cold and heavy snows to Buffalo Township. Then the Muir homestead was a lonely oasis in the midst of a vast desert of white. Not for over four miles could another settler's family be found. The wind howled through the trees, rustling the old, dried oak leaves; the lake was frozen. Jock, the pony, Tom and Jerry, the oxen, and the one new cow had been given shelter in the shanty. In the big house the cold was like a driving force, brutal and implacable. One small stove in the kitchen to fight it back, about which ten people huddled for warmth. One small firebox which held at most five sticks of wood. John thought of the fireplace which might have stood in the front room, in all the rooms for that matter, fireplaces like the good hot ones in Dunbar. He remembered the masses of wood which had been burned last spring as the trees were felled; remembered, and could not let himself think of it. But he decided, with a boy's wisdom, that it was stupid and wasteful, and kept the matter to himself.

Since he was the oldest boy, more and more of the chores of the farm fell on his shoulders. Father called him early now at the first, dim sign of daylight.

"Come on down, Johnny, and fetch the firewood!"

Shivering, barefooted, blowing on his freezing hands, John crept down the stairs. The shoes he had left under the stove last night, the soggy wool socks, had frozen stiff. He struggled to push his poor, chilblained feet into them. Though he longed for a little heat, Father had forbidden the starting of fire until the outside work was done.

Into the outdoor cold now, pulling the long, hand-knitted tippet over his head and about his neck. The wind tore at it, howling like a hundred banshees. When the stock had been fed and watered and the cow milked, there were water pails to be filled from the spring in the meadow. The first rays of the sun were slanting in fire across the snow as he climbed back up the slippery hill. Suddenly the dim land blazed in glory and he stood to look, forgetting the pain in his aching feet, the chills which shook him.

When he came in, Mother was wrestling with the stove in the misty kitchen. She had lighted one candle and the dim glow seemed to highlight the strain and weariness in her face. She had looked so bonnie when she first came! "Let me, Mother," he said, taking the firewood out of her hands. Now a merry crackling and delicious warm smells of coffee, Scotch oatmeal, American pancakes! Soon Margaret came, bringing the twins, wrapped up to their ears; then Father, saying it was time for prayers. The winter day had begun.

The long, bitter winter yielded to spring at last. Ice on the lake went out with a protesting boom and roar, to be followed by the wild, unearthly laughter of the loons. Bluebirds, thrushes, warblers, bobolinks, meadow larks, flocks of geese swept by and sometimes the high-riding swans, with their lonely bugle-like call. The burned-over patches of land were gay with purple anemones.

One day when John was prowling along the edge of the woods he heard a curious, buzzing roar like an oncoming wind. Suddenly a great flock of birds darkened the sky, rising, falling, alighting, flying on again, the rear becoming the leaders, the leaders dropping back to the rear, so that the whole seemed to revolve like a giant wheel. Red, green, gold, crimson, blue, the lovely colors seemed to fill the air; the sky was alive with wings. At once John knew with a quick inner excitement these were the birds he had read about so long ago. Surely these were the passenger pigeons which the great Audubon had described!

Later he stood watching Sarah as she plucked the limp, bedraggled bodies which his father had shot, and turned her piecrust with a deft hand. In this wilderness farm he was well used to killing. The fox must be shot to save the chickens; the squirrels must be killed to save the corn. But these . . . were different. Sarah felt his eyes upon her. As if he had spoken, she answered, "Aye, it's a pity. It's awfu' like a sin to kill the bonnie things!"

But Daniel, reading by the stove, looked up. "Nonsense, Sarah! God sent the creatures for us to eat, as he sent the quails to the Israelites when they were starving."

"But we're not starving, Father," said John, always ready for an argument. "Have they no right to live?"

With almost a passionate longing John had looked forward to spring, when he would be free again as he had been that first spring. Free to roam the woods, to ride Jock over the rounded hills, to fish in the lake. But John's father had other plans. The farm must be made to pay and John, as the oldest son, must carry his share of the load. From the time of his April birthday, when he had just turned twelve, the work of a man was thrust upon his shoulders.

First the spring plowing. Though his head barely reached above the great plow handles and he had to stretch up his arms to hold them, he was held to this work, hour on hour. At first the furrows snaked their way across the field, and, at the end of one, he could hardly manage the horse and turn the unwieldy plowshare. But soon he gained strength and skill. Now the furrows were straight and clean; he was proud of his work and the hired men praised him.

Planting seeds was more like fun, but oh, the hateful hoeing, row on row, when the fields of potatoes, corn, melons, wheat were ready. This was easy work, his father thought, sending Davie and even the girls out to constant, backbreaking toil. Worst of all, he forbade them to work together on the same row, lest they waste time in "idle tittle-tattle."

When the Muirs first came to Buffalo Township, they had no neighbors for four miles on any side. But soon the country began to fill up with land-hungry immigrants, seeking claims. Philip Gray of Edinburgh settled one mile south of the Muirs. His house became the first post office and soon the news was spread around that he was calling all settlers to help build a school. To John, who had been so happy last year to escape from study, this news seemed to offer a vision of freedom. Books! How he hungered for them now and longed to run away from the endless drudgery!

He approached his father a trifle cautiously. "Will you not help Mr. Gray build the new schoolhouse, Father?" and then he added wistfully, "Can I go to it, Father?"

Daniel looked back at his oldest son and his eyes were troubled. But he spoke firmly. "I can't spare you from the farm, Johnny. You're a good worker."

Soon another rumor came round. Philip Gray was starting a lending library in his home. This time John consulted no one. Early one morning after the chores were done, he bridled Jock and slipped away. When he came back, the saddlebags were bulging with strange shapes.

One day as John, Margaret, and Sarah were coming wearily back from the field for their noon lunch they saw a stranger walking up the corduroy road. Young, tall, with a thick crop of coal black hair, and eyes almost too blue in his browned and handsome face, he stepped over the slippery, uneven logs with a kind of easy grace.

"Will ye no tell me, Miss, where Mr. Muir lives?"

He seemed to be speaking to Sarah, who evidently liked the young man beside her, for she smiled as she looked up at him. "Come with us, sir. His home is just around the corner."

He smiled back then and, sensing the girl's weariness, put out a hand, took the hoe away from her, and swung it up soldierlike across one shoulder.

So, casually and without ceremony, David Galloway from Fifeshire, Scotland, came into the life of the Muirs.

Though John had mastered the art of swimming, and a lake stood at his door, there was little time in all that long, broiling summer to practise his skill. Called at four in the morning, he had the chores to do before breakfast —scythe sharpening, feeding animals, chopping stove-wood, fetching water. After breakfast, the hay or the harvest field, the long, dogged, breathless hours of mid-summer.

John, proud of his strength and his new-found man-hood, strained hard to keep in line with the hired men, strained far beyond the strength of a boy and there was no one wise enough to caution him against it. Rushing ahead in the wheat field, he swung the great scythe in a wide arc, feeling a sense of triumph as the golden grain fell before the fingers on his cradle. Margaret came stumbling behind him, stooping over to rake the loose grain, then holding it in her arms as she bound it into a bundle. The fields must be worked swiftly; the bundles must be hauled to the barn for threshing by the wooden flail with its eelskin thong. A sudden rain might destroy the crop.

At noon came an hour for rest and food and further chores; then back to the wheat field, often to toil until dark. Supper, the cows to fetch and milk, family prayers, then bed; a night that was far too short, an exhausted, dreamless sleep—over and over the days repeated the same pattern.

David Galloway came back often that summer, ap-

parently to call on Daniel, but it was plain that his real interest was in the children. Though he was nine years older than John, the black-haired Highlander soon became friends with the copper-haired boy who chased after him asking questions. But if David liked John, it was plain that he was even more partial to Sarah. One day, when he found her weak and dizzy in the wheat field, trying to help Margaret bind the wheat, he swept her up into his arms and carried her home. Later he faced Daniel with blazing eyes.

"Man, will ye make slaves of the women, too?" he asked and added more gently, "I'll give ye what help I can today, Daniel!"

After weeks of searching, David Galloway told Sarah he had found the land he wished and staked a claim to eighty acres. Land for his father he found in another township to the north. Now he must go back to the Old Country to bring his family over.

"And then, no doubt, I'll be choosing me a wife!" He looked at Sarah with a gleam in his eyes and a smile, half teasing, half tender. To her disgust, she felt the warm glow rising to her cheeks, but she answered lightly, "Plenty of old maids around, David!"

Several days later, when David came to say good-by, he drew Sarah a little apart from the rest. "Well, my own lassie, it's farewell at last—but not for long," he cried as he saw the tears in her eyes.

"So far away!" she said, brushing at the tears with a quick hand, "So very dangerous!"

"When I come back, you'll be woman grown."

"I'm a woman now," she answered, with a proud toss of the head. Then, as she knew the meaning of her words, the tormenting flush rose up over her cheeks again to the edges of her hair. "I'm most fifteen!"

"Fifteen—and so good and pretty." He stooped to kiss her, but gently, not possessively. With a final wave, he strode away.

John, who came by shortly afterwards, to find Sarah crying bitterly, put out his hand and squeezed hers. For once he did not try to tease her.

3

Back-Country Things

FOR FIVE YEARS THE "WEE PONY, JOCK" WAS JOHN'S
great companion and friend. No question but that there
was an understanding between them. Jock whinnied in
welcome if John so much as set foot in the stable; free
in the pasture, he came running when John moved the
first bar of the gate. In the morning, doing his chores,
John fed him first; at night, the last pat went to Jock.

A staunch little horse that never balked at anything,
the wild boys early taught him to jump. It was great fun
to clear the small brooks in a smooth leap and land on
the rough ground without a spill! In the late summer
afternoons either Davie or John rounded up the cows on
Jock's back, and now the pony had developed a bad habit
which enraged Daniel. If the boys were so much as a
minute late, some inner time sense seemed to send Jock
off; he cleared the pasture bars and went for the cows
alone.

"It must not happen again! The beastie has the De'il
in him. 'Twill be the ruin of the cattle!" How often

Daniel had proclaimed this in his most solemn manner!
It never occurred to John that he really meant it.

It was a late August afternoon when John was seventeen. Bars of rose and gold stood in the western sky; a
vesper sparrow gave its lovely, haunting song. With his
usual shrill whistle John neared the pasture, but no eager
whinny came to answer him. To his dismay, he realized
that "wee Jockie" had stolen the march again.

A long hill led down from the upper farm to the corral.
Now the sound of pounding hoofs, the complaint of
cattle, could be plainly heard, as Jock walloped the protesting herd in a dead run down to the stable below.
Frisky and competent, he galloped from side to side, nip-
ping their flanks, turning back the strays, holding the
ranks, while the unfortunate cows, with their udders
shaking and their tails on end, tore on, as if the "De'il"
were indeed after them.

Daniel, watching beside the stable door, was outraged
beyond endurance. "John—*John!*" he called with an
angry emphasis there was no mistaking.

"Aye, Father?"

"I'll have this no more, John. Go get your gun!"

"My—my gun, Father?"

"Aye. *You must shoot Jock!*"

John felt as if an icy hand had clutched at his heart.
Shoot Jock—the one pet which he loved best in all the
world, the little horse his father had given him when he
first came here—it was unthinkable! The moment was

unreal. But there was no relenting in his father's angry eyes.

Without a word he swung around and started back toward the house. He was a Scot, trained through years in the habit of complete obedience. How could he defy his father?

Ann Muir sat sewing in her front parlor, swaying back and forth in the big rocker, singing softly to herself. At the sight of John's tense, strained look she let the homespun in her hands flutter to the ground.

"Laddie, what's wrong?" she cried, jumping to her feet.

Wordless, he marched past her, went into the kitchen and, going to the wall rack where the guns lay stretched on wooden pegs, took his down and turned. She stood before him with outstretched hands, anxiety in her eyes.

"Can't you tell your own mother?"

He started to speak, choked suddenly, and tried again. "Mother . . . I . . . Father says . . . I must kill Jock."

"Kill Jock? Oh, no!" The horror in her voice matched the anguish of his own heart. Then, seizing his arm, she cried, "I'll come with you."

"No, Mother. You stay here." Swiftly he strode away.

He stood facing his father now, the gun in one hand, his blue eyes hard as steel. Daniel led Jock forward, fastening him to an outside stanchion of the barn. The pony pawed the ground, flattened his ears, and pulled back against the lead rope, as if aware of impending danger. John could bear it no longer. When the little horse turned his head and looked at him, a great wave of anger swept over him. The words rushed out in a torrent; with blazing eyes he crashed his gun to the ground and left it there.

"I care not one bit what you do to me, or what you say . . . I'll never kill Jock . . . never, never, never!"

Before his father could answer, before he could do anything to stop him, John swung around and marched away, thinking for a moment that he heard the rustle of his mother's skirts behind him. Fleet as an Indian, he ran toward the woods.

When John came back that night, leaving at last his sanctuary of the forest, he found that Jock had not been killed. For tactful Ann, quietly cajoling her husband, had talked him into reason. "No," he had admitted, a calculating look in his eyes, " 'twould not be so very canny to shoot such a good horse, young, strong, well-gaited."

The next day Daniel disappeared on the road to Portage, leading the pony behind him. When he returned, two new work horses, Nob and Nell, were added to the stable. All that John ever learned was that Jock had been sold to a man who would ride him to California. Many a night, twisting and turning, as sleep would not come, he wondered how the little horse fared. Was he hungry, cruelly used, hard-driven, or had he fallen into kind and careful hands? Even at the end of his life John Muir once wrote, "I still wish I knew what had become of Jock."

* * *

It was the spring of 1856, about five years from the time when David Galloway had said good-by to the Muirs. Sarah was standing in the heat of June, hoeing down a row between the spears of corn. How long she had waited for him, she thought, but now—it all began to seem like a dream!

Then suddenly she saw him, coming down the row, coming as simply as he had the first time, conquering space in an instant, standing beside her with all the old power and charm. But she had turned into a tongue-tied schoolgirl, unable to look up, unable to speak, acting like a foolish clown.

"Sarah, darling," he said, "can't you look at me? I'm not so very much changed!"

Then she was laughing, though her lips were trembling; and her hands were in his and the old electric thrill came from them, straight to her heart.

Later, David had many a serious word with Sarah's mother, who greeted him warmly, as if he were a returning son.

"Why is Sarah so thin and pale, ma'am? Is she ill?"

"Just now the work is extra hard, David. John is needed at the other farm and his father is away."

"The other farm?"

"Aye, Daniel has bought himself a new acreage."

"Leaving you and the children, without John, to carry on all the work here?"

" 'Tis as you say, David—and very hard on all of us!"

"Hard and unfair, ma'am," David Galloway cried bluntly. Later he pressed his suit vigorously.

"How soon may I marry Sarah, Mother Muir? I've waited a long five years."

"It is needful to consult Daniel," Ann Muir answered. "He must give his consent. But there'll be no doubt about it," she added with a mischievous smile.

When John and Sarah went to meet David's mother, she seemed to take an instant fancy to them both and they were impressed by the old lady, with the Gaelic shawl over her shoulders. It was John's hand she clung to longest, to his great embarrassment.

"Aye, the Gordon blood," she said, " 'Tis plain enough!"

Slowly her discerning eyes roved over him, to note the rumpled copper-colored hair, the brilliant blue eyes beneath it, the sensitive mouth and stubborn chin, the lean, strong, thin-waisted body, not too tall, the muscles rippling under his faded shirt. A colt that will travel far, aye—very far, she thought to herself. Aloud she asked, "What be the knobby things in your pockets, John?"

"Oh, these?" said John, pulling out an odd collection —bits of hickory of queer shapes and sizes, handmade nails, knives, an old corset steel. "I'm fashioning a fine-tooth saw that cuts the hardest wood. We didn't have one."

"Why do you need it?"

"Oh, I'm working on a self-setting sawmill, and I have in mind some kind of a new-fangled clock."

"A clock? But that's very sagacious! Have you seen the insides of one?"

"No, but I imagine how it'll be."

"Amazing!" said Jean Galloway firmly. "Ye'll go far, young man, ye'll go far!"

But why, John wondered, had he told the old lady about these things? He never talked about his inventions. Seeing his embarrassment, David pulled him away.

"You mustn't mind Mother! Like many a Highlander, she's a bit fey."

"I like her," said John firmly, and meant it with all his heart. Later, the understanding and sympathy which he found in David's mother became one of the formative influences of his life.

In December the snows were deep when Sarah and David stood up to be married, but the warmth and happiness in their hearts defied all cold and storm. Now the house which Sarah had watched building in this wilderness place, became her very own, for Daniel Muir and David Galloway agreed to exchange their holdings. Now she was mistress of Fountain Lake Farm and, from that time on, she never worked in the fields again.

John Muir could hardly remember when the passion to read had not been part of his life. How else could a boy so lonely learn about the world? "The Bible is all ye need to know, Johnny!" Daniel told him. But John had already found Cowper, Milton, Shakespeare, Sir Walter Scott; in their company the drudgery of his days seemed to fade away. But the right to read and the time to read had to be passionately defended. A few minutes at noon before he went back to the field; a few minutes after supper before his father sent him to bed, scraps of time so needed, so fought for. Yet in the last summer, John managed to take himself through higher arithmetic, geometry, trigonometry, to give himself the education he had been denied. He had found in a book the time laws of the pendulum, and started trying to build the wonderful clocks of which he dreamed. Then at last came the great chance!

"Johnny!"

"Aye, sir!"

"It be eight o'clock, Johnny. Time for bed."

"Oh, Father, just a few wee minutes more."

"Johnny, you're a long-tongued child! Come, obey me!"

Slowly John rose, thumping the covers of his book together, a boy of seventeen, treated like a baby! Perhaps at last the misery in his eyes did move his father.

"If you wish so much to read, Johnny, get up in the morning as early as you like. I've no objection."

When he crawled beneath the quilts in his icy bedroom, John planned to stay awake all night, but fatigue took care of that. Soundly he slept—until . . . With great excitement he jumped up, noting the deep darkness about him. How much time had he won? On aching, chilblained feet he crept down the stairs, holding a tallow dip up to the clock on the kitchen wall. One o'clock only. Five hours early. He had won five whole hours to do with as he wished!

At first he planned to read, looking wistfully at the bits of wood in the kindling box. No, Father would never forgive this needless waste of fuel. Soon he plunged down into the cellar and began to work on the self-setting saw-mill with which he had long been tinkering. His fingers ached with cold. The dim light of a single candle sent queer shadows flickering across the stones. But happiness was a cloak of warmth about him. He had won five hours of freedom; there would be other nights beyond this and beyond. Already he was rich above his wildest dreams.

So the same work had to be done all over again, the hard and bitter drudgery of turning wild, new land into a cultivated farm! Why had Father brought this burden upon them? John stood at the top of Hickory Hill and let his eyes wander downward over the country below. A lovely view and a sightly spot for a home. No wonder Father had chosen it, and yet . . .

He thought wistfully of the land to which they had first come, Fountain Lake Farm, six miles to the north-west. How long ago it seemed! He had loved the gleaming little lake, ringed with pond lilies, the wild brook where he had had such fun with his sawmill. This place had no water, not so much as a brook or spring. "Ye must dig a well," William Duncan, their new neighbor, had told them. "Aye," his father had answered, letting his eyes rest thoughtfully on his oldest son. From that moment John had been well aware who was to do the dig-ging!

He stood now a few minutes longer, gazing at the sun-lit land below him. He noted the raucous call of a blue jay, the long murmur of the wind, as it came blowing over miles of forest. His thoughts seemed to ride the wind to distant places, to other times. "Free as the wind." Would he himself ever be free?

John stooped to lift the ax which he had left leaning against the trunk of an oak tree. This was his work and he must be getting on with it! If he had his way, he thought, glancing up along the gnarled trunk into the wide, witchlike branches of the oak above him, he would never chop down another tree. Surely it was the devil's work to ruin something which stood so beautiful in its age and power! How he hated the long, sighing shudder with which a big tree fell. So long in growing, so quick to die! He looked at the trampled earth about him, at the rough slash, half-chopped trunks of trees already cut, the piled-up heaps of discarded branches. With a sudden burning sense of anger he lifted his ax for the first blow.

Early in the summer, when the Muirs were planning to move to Hickory Hill, the problem of the well came up again. As John had guessed, it became his task to sink the bore. The first ten feet were quickly dug down through soft earth and loam. Then his shovel struck sand-stone and a day's chipping with hammer and mason's chisels seemed to gain hardly an inch.

He faced his father that night, a tall, thin lad, exhausted

by fruitless work. He was dripping with sweat, stained brown by the dust of the earth, discouraged and grim.

"I can't make headway, Father!" He threw his tools clattering to the ground.

"Nonsense, laddie! You're a good worker. Tomorrow 'twill go better!" Daniel's unctuous voice tried to sound soothing. Once John would have glowed with joy under his father's praise. Now he knew it for what it was—the lure to slavery.

As he turned away, John caught sight of William Duncan's red oxen slowly swinging their way up the hill; soon their neighbor stood beside him. With shrewd glance he looked from father to son, then marched to the edge of the bore and stood regarding it. Stonemason and miner for many years in Scotland, he read at once the story of John's day.

"Daniel, did you know the folk hereabouts say, 'Farmer Muir works his children like beasts'?"

"Whisht, Duncan! God's work ne'er hurt man nor child!"

"An' what if 'twere the De'il's work?" Gruffly he swung about, saying, "'Tis only dynamite will soften stone." Ignoring Daniel, he laid a kindly hand on John's shoulder. "Coom to my house soon, Johnny! I've a new book for ye."

Perhaps moved by Duncan, John's father tried once or twice to use blasting. Not knowing how to control it and being afraid of it, he soon threw the task back into John's hands.

Day after day, week after week through the hot summer, shut up in an airless shaft three feet in diameter, John chipped his way deeper and deeper down through the rock. Every morning Daniel and Davie lowered him in a bucket turned by a windlass, hauled him up for food at noon, then lowered him until dark. Cramped and miserable, shut away from sunlight and air, his legs bent, his arms aching, he slowly worked his way downward.

For several mornings he had felt a queer faintness when he first found himself at the bottom of the shaft. Now came the moment when his candle-lantern went out suddenly, as the bucket bumped downward. Climbing out on the floor of the well, he began to pick up the chips, left the day before, but the bits of stone slipped through his fingers. Nausea seized him. His head swam, a black vertigo sent him reeling back against the bucket, clutching it for support. Just as his last control seemed slipping away, he managed to look up the long, dark shaft to the very top. Yes, there was the sunshine, the gleaming leaves of a burr oak branch shining across the well top. Back, back again to sunlight! Briefly, as if he were drowning, he thought of the scootchers of his childhood, of that dreadful moment long ago in the dungeon of Dunbar Castle. Someway he must muster his strength—and escape.

"Father," he called feebly, "Father, take me out!"

Daniel, who was watching John's descent, had been troubled. Why had the candle flickered and died? Now he heard the weak cry and was frightened.

"Get back into the bucket, Johnny," he shouted. "*Get back in!*"

They pulled him up at last and carried him away all but unconscious, gasping from the deadly chokedamp.

"And 'tis God's mercy the laddie didn't die!" William Duncan told the neighbors.

At the top of the hill, on the site which John had cleared, the new house was soon standing. It was well made with careful craftsmanship; strong hand-hewn beams upheld it and fine white plaster was laid upon its walls. It had two stories and an attic above that. On the ground floor there were parlor, buttery, kitchen, and a small bedroom which Daniel had planned as his own retreat. But he had reckoned without his oldest son.

Just below the bedroom was a stonewalled cellar with a storm door entering it from the outside. Remembering his early rising permission, John chose this cavelike place for his own refuge. Here, curled up like a hibernating bear, he half lay, half squatted on the stone floor, his back against a wooden apple bin, his eyes on the candle-lit book before him. Now one hand turned the pages; now he thrust it into the bin behind him. Soon rhythmic munching broke the silence. From the room above came the sound of snoring. All was peace between father and son. But not for long.

Weary of reading, John reached for his hammer and nails, bits of hickory, discarded scraps of metal, old corset stays. Soon he was hard at work on the latest of his dreams, a clock that could "do everything." If it looked more like a sawmill than a clock, who cared? It was to tell the time, the days of the week and month, light fires, and by a series of cogs and levers to be attached to a rough bed it was to tip the bed and turn the sleeper out at any hour he wished. Oh, wonderful clock! Some day he would have it finished.

Now the scream of tortured metal, the sharp clank, clank, clank of hammer upon nail began to drift up to the sleeping Daniel. He twisted and stared into the darkness. John! Who else? The very De'il's in the laddie, he thought. But then he remembered. He had given his word to his son that he "might read or work as early as he wished." How could he, a Scotsman, go back on his word? So John continued to "fill his wisdom bins," as he liked to say, and more than one invention was born in that cave of a cellar on Hickory Hill.

It was the winter when John was nineteen. What magic word or argument he managed to use that persuaded Daniel to let him go to school, even his mother never knew. But go he did for three whole months, the only time he had seen a school since his days at the schools in Scotland. But as suddenly as it had begun, John's new schooling came to an end. "Needed on the farm," was his father's tight-lipped decision; at the end of three months he was forced to leave the Eddy school; nor did he ever see it again.

In these days of heartbreak, with the door closed tight against his learning, John turned eagerly to his "nonsensical whittling." Through stolen hours of night and early morning he bent over his tools and a wonderful clock evolved, made in the shape of a scythe to show the ruthless cutting of Father Time. The pendulum was formed like a bunch of arrows. The whole was fastened to a leafless oak branch and upon it was carved the mournful reflection, "All Flesh is Grass." Of this clock, with its Biblical message, Daniel approved. But when he found his son designing a huge affair with four dials and a two-second pendulum, fourteen feet long, meant to be set on the top of the barn roof, where it could be seen from any direction, even by neighbors working in the fields, his patience was gone.

"Will ye bring every prying busybody to this farm?" he roared. Already he was having enough of the curiosity seekers, who came to gape at John's inventions. Some went away shaking their heads and saying the lad was daft, but others, like William Duncan, marveled at his untaught skill, spreading the news far and wide that he was a true genius, who would go "very far."

The weeks passed, days of toil and nights when John could retreat into his secret world, surrounded by darkness and the quiet of the cellar. But even his whittling, happy escape though it was, hardly satisfied him now. For he faced the stark fact that soon he would be of age, able to go where he wished and do what he wanted. Where would he go? What could he do? As yet there was no answer. He was uneducated, untaught, except as a farm helper, used in every random job, trained in none.

Once he had asked his father timidly whether there might be a little money to help him reach medical school. The answer was stony silence.

Something—somewhere? Perhaps a machine shop would be the answer, where his nimble fingers could handle the tools he liked. Everywhere men were drifting away from Wisconsin farms to find work in industry; to factories in Chicago, Indianapolis, Milwaukee, Detroit. This was the dawn of the machine age.

Well, he could join the procession, be lost in the turmoil and confusion, slave to the machine, as he had been slave to the land!

In April, 1859, John came of age. He was free! But still he lingered on at home, hating to go, hating to leave Margaret, who was now his closest friend, his mother whom he loved, Davie and Danny, Joanna, the spoiled, amusing little sister.

It was the summer of 1860. John was like a young hawk, trying his wings on the edge of the nest, stretching them, balancing, stumbling back into security and shelter. Night after night he tossed in his bed, while his head ached and his veins were a throbbing fire. All the demon worries came to torment him. Where could he go? Was his life useless and the future without meaning?

It was midnight, one o'clock, two o'clock, three. The little timepiece on the kitchen shelf chimed the hours. Unable to bear it longer, John slipped from bed, stole softly away from the airless bedroom, and wandered out under the stars.

He climbed down into a deep ravine north of the house and, expert in the darkness, he found a swift way up the opposite side. The slight cracking of a twig made him stop; he found that the old collie, with a dog's sure instinct for human need, was following him.

Now he came to a place he loved, a grove of tall, white pines, mysterious in the faint light. He threw himself on his back, stretching his arms out along the ground above his head and the collie lay down beside him. High above him, beyond the dim, shadowy fretwork of the branches, he saw the shifting light of stars.

What? Where? When? All the old, vexing questions began to come and bedevil him, but suddenly they seemed petty and unimportant. With a long sigh of peace and contentment, he let them slip away.

It was September. Already there was a touch of red and gold in the forest when William Duncan came calling at the Muir farm.

"Wonderful! 'Tis beyond belief!" he was saying, as he examined a big outdoor thermometer which John had fastened to the wall of the farmhouse. "Why, even the heat of the body makes it show a change."

"Oh, aye!" Daniel answered casually, while John smiled at the words of obvious admiration.

"Johnny!" With a slap of his hand on John's back, the old stonemason turned to speak to him. "Do you know in a week or two 'twill be fair time at Madison? The great State Agricultural Fair will be showing there for all the world to see. Everything, from heifers to—women's quilts. Couldn't ye pack up your inventions and take them? Any shop in the place would give you a job, if they saw your contraptions."

A flush climbed John's face, erasing the freckles, while his eyes gleamed. "Back-country things, made of wood, is there any hope? They wouldn't look at them, I'm afraid."

"Nonsense! Pack up your things and give yourself a chance, Johnny!"

4

Independence— for What?

JOHN STOOD JINGLING THE COINS IN HIS POCKET AS HE waited before the admissions window of the great state fair at Madison. Few enough they were! Would the entrance fee ruin him? First the gold piece that Grandfather Gilrye had given him so long ago. Then the little money he had earned by raising wheat on that barren land that Father had abandoned. Well, at least it was his own!

Before him the waiting line inched slowly forward. Around him the throng of people shouted and jostled. Soldiers in uniform, barkers calling their wares, farmers bearing exhibits, men top-hatted and elegant, ladies with great swinging hoop skirts, workmen in shirt sleeves carrying boards and tools. A confused, disturbing, fascinating scene to a lad from the back country. The chaos of voices seemed to join, to be part of the shimmering September heat, the dust that filled his nostrils, the loud, martial blare of bands, above which came the thin, tortured wail of a calliope.

"Well, what in thunder have we here?"

The kindly face peering down from the admissions booth seemed to notice at once the bundle across John's back and addressed the question to it.

"Oh, some machines I have invented, sir, to exhibit . . . I hope."

"What kind of machines?"

"Oh—well—two clocks, a sort of early-rising machine —a thermometer."

"Humph! So that's all, is it! Come right in, young feller, you don't need a ticket."

For a while John wandered, watching the crowds, savoring the excitement. Now a lane of side shows, with a giant swing for the children; a tent adorned with pictures of writhing serpents, where the lady snake charmer sat and fanned herself. Now the great agricultural tent and the floral tent; pens of poultry, sheep, cows, bulls, horses; aisles filled with exhibits—squashes, pumpkins, cheeses, apples, flowers. One great golden squash, weighing one hundred and forty-two pounds, as its placard proudly proclaimed.

At last John questioned a man who looked official.

"Clocks, is it? See that big place on a hill where the flag's wavin'? That's the Fine Arts Hall. Try there!"

Again John faced officialdom, an impressive gentleman with stylish coattails. Conscious suddenly of his own shirt sleeves, bedraggled wisp of a coat, braces that held up a pair of shapeless trousers, he still managed to summon a hopeful smile.

Professor Daniel Read, head of the department of English literature of the University of Wisconsin, looked with amazement at the lean, broad-shouldered lad who stood so patiently before him. He noted the drab country clothes, the unkempt tangle of tawny hair, and the puckish streak of soot over one eyebrow, where a recent train ride had left its mark.

"You have an exhibit?" he questioned, but his uncertainty changed to wonder when he saw the unusual, beautiful clocks unpacked before him. "Any place you wish," he promised. "Look around and select your own corner. We'll give you a carpenter to make the shelving. We don't have things as original as this come our way often!"

All that day and the next John's head was in a whirl, his heart pounding with excitement. Out on the edge of the grounds he found two boulders to use as weights and soon had his beloved contraptions in fine running order. The clock that looked like a scythe stood on a handsome shelf, impressive as it boomed out the hours. The thermometer was hung nearby. Soon his trick bed was roughed together, two legs at the top and one at the bottom. The single leg held up a jointed crosspiece in which a key peg was placed. From the peg a cord was run to an escapement device on a clock. At the time set, this wheel on the clock turned with a whirr, drawing taut the cord, which pulled out the peg. Now with a creak and a jolt, the foot of the bed fell down, leaving the sleeper at an angle of forty-five degrees, until finally he found himself on the floor.

A great attraction John found his early-rising machine

to be. Everyone stood around and gaped at it, as he set it up, asking questions, offering free advice. Two friendly women loaned him blankets. Now all was complete, save for the needed sleeper. Who would be willing to give a demonstration of falling out on the floor?

Fortunately, at this point the man in charge of admissions appeared with a lady and two small boys in tow. "Mr. Muir, let me introduce you to Mrs. Ezra Carr, who is one of our special committee members for the fair. And here are Harry Butler and Mrs. Carr's son."

"I am honored, ma'am!" said John, with his quick, engaging smile, liking the little woman who smiled back at him. "Howdy, fellers!" he added and solemnly shook hands with each of the boys. Then, suddenly inspired, he asked, "Are either of you laddies particularly good at falling out of bed?"

From that time on John's success was complete. The news of the trick bed spread far and wide. The curious group about it became a crowd, the crowd grew to a pushing throng. Singly or together the boys fell out, after a peaceful interval of snoring. Sometimes they chose to land on their feet, but at last, with great enthusiasm, slid out on their heads. The joy of the small fry, the sly humor and pride of the inventor, the cleverness of the machine, plus the uproarious response of the crowd, made John Muir's invention the great attraction of the hall.

Next day, to his vast surprise, John found that two leading newspapers had given front page space to his exhibit.

"*Wisconsin State Journal*, Sept. 25th, 1860," he read.

AN INGENIOUS WHITTLER. While at the Fair Grounds this morning we saw some very ingenious specimens of mechanism in the form of clocks, made by Mr. John Muir of Buffalo, Marquette Co. . . . We will venture to predict that few articles will attract as much attention as these products of Mr. Muir's ingenuity.

Along with notices of "highbred, game-looking fowls, venerable old rams, monstrously fat and clean-looking pigs," The *Evening Patriot* wrote, The Temple of Art contained plenty of sewing machines and the show of fancy articles was being increased by constant arrivals. We noticed here *two great curiosities in the shape of some wooden clockwork,* which was in motion, and the cogwheels and all the woodwork about it had been cut out of wood by the young man from Marquette County who is with it. The work is surprising and could only have been executed by genuine genius.

"Genuine genius, genuine genius"—the words seemed to blur before John's eyes. Never let Father learn of this or a letter full of preachments would come his way!

John thought of his father with regret. As he left, he had asked him cautiously whether, if he was ever in dire straits, he might turn to him for a little help. "No, depend entirely upon yourself," Daniel had answered.

"You'll find strangers will be unkind and rude, John!"
he had added encouragingly. But it was the strangers who
seemed kind, Daniel who had been thoughtless. He could
see his father now, as he refused to say good-by to his
eldest son, turning on his heel to march away.

How much John wished that the fair would never end!
To be the center of attraction, to savor the excitement
and praise—this was a heady brew for a lad from a lonely
farm. Once again the demon question rose to plague him.
Where could he go? What could he do? How could he
meet the future?

One more pleasure fate held in store for him. The fair
ended with awards and prizes. The little lady who had
come to see his exhibit, whose son had been a lively and
hilarious partner, was judge on a committee to decide
about the "irregular exhibits." John found himself
awarded fifteen dollars and a diploma, which spoke again
of his genius.

Packing up his inventions, he slung them across his
back and went to view once more the place that held the
real attraction for him, the university campus joining the
fair grounds. He wandered over the beautiful lawns,
through lanes of towering elm trees, stopping to gaze at
Main Hall, at North Hall where men students lived, at
Lake Mendota gleaming through the trees. Far, far below,
at the bottom of the hill on which he stood, he saw the
shining dome of the Capitol.

John's heart held only envy as he watched the students
strolling by, so much at home. He longed to stay. If only

—he thought. For a moment he dreamed that he belonged here, too, a freshman hurrying to some science class. Then he shrugged away the dream and wandered on. But as he left the beautiful campus with its great arching trees, something staunch inside him answered, "Aweel—no doubt I'll be back!"

One other exhibit at the fair had attracted even more attention than those of John Muir. This was the *Lady Franklin*, a great iceboat, shown by "Wiard the Wizard," an inventor from New Jersey.

John saw the throngs gaping at the big, flat-bottomed boat. He heard the admiration and praise. "Greater than Stephenson, greater even than Robert Fulton." He was flattered when Norman Wiard came to see his own work, offering him, by the end of the fair, a chance to help him in his foundry. After his last wistful glance at the university, John wandered back to the fair grounds just in time to find the *Lady Franklin* being hoisted on to a huge truck.

"Well, are you coming, Muir? We'll ride the *Lady* to Prairie du Chien!"

The ride in the baggage car of the train, sitting on a thwart of the iceboat, was great fun for John Muir. But when he found that the foundry was only a cheap shack, hung with cobwebs and thick with dirt, he was disturbed. He soon found that Norman Wiard was almost never on hand, that he himself was little but a chore boy, kept to polish, clean, and guard the one and only exhibit.

The days went by. Winter came to this port city on

the Mississippi. To keep himself from starving, John found a job with an Irishman named Grogan, milking his cow, feeding his horse, in return for a few meals. The townspeople began to clamor for a trial run. The ice thickened on the great river and Wiard could refuse no longer. But *Lady Franklin* gave one great choking cough, then settled down firmly on the ice, inert and useless. "A small repair job," Norman Wiard promised. "She'll run the next time."

Soon John captured a new job more to his liking. Hired as man of all work at the Mondell House, the leading hotel of Prairie du Chien, he found himself welcomed by a pleasant family. Mr. and Mrs. Pelton, the owners, early sensed the quality of this lad from the back country. They gave him more and more responsibility and made him feel at home. And Emily, the niece, a charming teenager with lovely oval face and big brown eyes, became his friend. "You're so much like Sarah," John told her, "though of course she's older!"

It was not long before the two of them went everywhere together, whenever they were free. Emily seemed to mean home and friendship. She was like one of his own sisters, but strangely more than a sister. She met his moods with understanding and his pulses were stirred by her loveliness.

The weeks wore on. Again the *Lady Franklin* failed in a new trial and the temper of the people turned nasty. John, who had tried to stand by and help the inventor, realized that he had been duped from the beginning.

Much as he hated to leave the shelter of the Mondell House, or to say good-by to Emily, John knew that this was a blind alley from which he must retreat. Moved by a sudden impulse, he went to the station and boarded a train for Madison. It was the end of January, 1861, when he returned to the university town where he had met his first triumph. But how different this was from fair time! Footsore and hungry, he tramped the streets looking for a job, to find one at last as coachman to a rich family named Hastings. Here he was slighted and half starved, an odd experience for a proud Scotsman! Whenever he could, he escaped to his dream world, the campus, beautiful in its winter snow, where at least he could pretend that he belonged.

One day, as he stood gazing up at the gray stone walls of North Hall a student came out the door, ran lightly down the steps, and hurried past him. Then he swung about, his strapful of books slapping at his thigh.

"Hey! Aren't you the fellow at the fair?"

"The fair? Yes, I was there!"

"I mean the fellow with the wonderful trick bed?"

"Well, yes. I did have one to exhibit."

"Say, you were great! And those two boys that fell out on their heads—Proffy Butler's son was one of them —didn't they love it?"

"They certainly did," said John, laughing.

"What are you doing now?"

"Wishing I was here at the university—but . . ."

"What's the matter?"

"No preparation and no money," John cried, looking grim and weary.

"Doesn't take much money, believe me. You can board yourself, you know. Pat'll let you bake potatoes in the furnace. Just a few dollars down for tuition. Why don't you go to see Proffy Butler, the father of your trick sleeper?"

"Is he the President?"

"Gad, no! We haven't any. Dean Sterling's the acting chancellor. You'll find him in Main Hall. Well, I'm late for class—hope you make it—see you later!"

The friendly student vanished along the path, and John, still clutching at his new, almost incredible hope, made a sudden decision. Go today, he thought. You'll go and put in your application now, while you're still in the mood, while you still have the courage. *You'll go now.*

Professor John Sterling, seated in the chancellor's office of the main building, bowed his head over a cluttered desk. He was discouraged and weary, baffled by all the burdens of leadership as acting chancellor. "Acting"—yes! The work, without the salary of a real president and without the glory.

And now this war, this senseless, useless, bloody waste of men and money. Already the students were melting away, throwing down their books and taking to arms. Soon there would be only women left to teach—and no funds for that.

A sudden, sharp rap came at his door, and he raised his head to see a tall young man standing there, a broad-shouldered man in an ill-fitting gray suit, but with such a light of eagerness in his face that he was moved by it. Hardly understanding his own impulse, he rose and stretched out a welcoming hand.

"Well, come in, sir! What may I do for you?"

"Dean Sterling?"

"Yes."

"I'm John Muir from up Portage way."

"Ah, a Scotsman, I take it," the chancellor answered, liking the pleasant accent, the deep, rumbling burr.

"Yes, sir. I wish very much to enter the university."

"Preparation?"

"Almost none, sir, that is, since I left Scotland at the age of eleven. Up to then I had good, hard schooling. With the aid of the Scotch 'tawse,'" he added with a smile.

"Have you done any work by yourself?"

"Oh, aye, sir, I've studied all my life, whenever I could get the books—geography, arithmetic, geometry, trigonometry . . ."

"And general reading?"

"The Bible, Shakespeare, Humboldt, the great German explorer, Scott, of course. I love the poets—Spenser, Chaucer, Cowper, Milton. Most and best of all, sir, Bobbie Burns!"

"Not a bad list," said Chancellor Sterling dryly. "Just some of the great books of the world!"

By the end of the interview, John Muir found that he was to be accepted "on trial." Some weeks or months in the preparatory department; then, when he was ready for it, he would be a member of the freshman class. When he left the room, John Sterling shook him warmly by the hand, surprised by the vigorous, muscular grip which almost crushed his own.

"Good-by, Mr. Muir, we'll welcome you with pleasure."

Now he could turn back to those confounded papers with something like zest. After all, it was a fine job! As long as young men like that came to him, to put their futures in his hands, it was a job worth doing.

To John, walking away from Main Hall, it seemed that he had been welcomed to a place "near, if not next to the Kingdom of Heaven."

Looking back on his few short years at college, John said he remembered it as a time when he was always happy—and always hungry. The first was exaggeration, but the last was truth, for it was not as easy as the friendly student had said to board oneself on next to nothing a week.

When the meager sum he earned as a coachman was spent for tuition and textbooks, what was left for food? John Muir had one answer. He picked up a chore or two, earned enough to keep himself alive, tightened his belt and, for the rest, thought of other things. Lean, spare, muscular, and strong, he already knew the rigorous ways of self-discipline. Bread and molasses, mush, potatoes which Pat, the janitor, let him bake in the ashes of the wood-burning furnace and an occasional gift of apples—

this was about all. Sometimes, reduced to fifty cents a week, he lived on milk and a handful of graham crackers. That his health was not ruined by such a diet was perhaps due to the contentment of his mind and his joy at being where he was. Now he could learn—so many things he longed to understand! At last that far more basic hunger of the spirit was satisfied.

For a few weeks John Muir stayed in the preparatory department till the faculty discovered where he stood, what work he could do. There was little question of his fitness for study. It was not long before he was listed as a regular member in good standing with the other Freshmen.

Happy that he had reached a longed-for goal, John seemed deaf and blind to the changes around him. Nose in a book, or trying his strength on the playground in a wrestling match or game of wicket, he let the world wag and gave little heed to the march of events. He had been brought up in a small, isolated place, shut in and away from national problems or political squabbles. But this was a time when the college was tense and insecure, the state rocked with excitement, the whole nation torn with a terrible anguish. This was April, 1861. The guns had spoken at Fort Sumter. The long fuse of hatred burning underground had burst at last into the red-hot flame of war.

Only half a mile away from the campus, the fair grounds, where John had shown his exhibits, were turned into an emergency training center called Camp Randall.

Here over seventy thousand men would be drilled and mobilized during the coming years. In his little northeast corner room on the second floor of North Hall, John Muir heard many of the sounds brought by this wild and hasty mustering. The tramp of marching feet, men's voices raised in song, the exciting call of fife and drum. But in writing home, once only he referred to "noises, common and uncommon," heard from his room, but added, "The thrushes in the pine grove don't seem to care. They whistle just as they do on the black and burr oaks at Hickory Hill. I always keep my window open, so I can hear them fine."

From the first John was welcomed into the college life. This, the dawn of the machine age, was a time when mechanical genius was rated high. John's reputation at the fair had gone ahead of him. The student he had so casually met and his two young partners greeted him as a long-lost friend. Other students visited his room, were amazed at his contraptions, and came under the spell of his charm.

They saw that he was poor, badly dressed, but completely unself-conscious; that his thick, tawny hair was rarely cut, that he kept his one good suit for special occasions only, but they also found that he was a magnificent swimmer, played a mean game of wicket, and could make the rest of them "eat dirt" at mumblety-peg.

Professor Butler and Professor Carr also discovered John Muir. Like their sons, they were glad to welcome him to their homes, rejoicing in a student who was hungry for what they had to give. Briefly John studied Latin and Greek under Butler. But though he soon gave up the classics, his warm admiration for the man who taught them lasted all his life.

Professor Carr, teacher of chemistry and geology, lighted a spark in John, soon fanned into a steady flame. He became the outstanding chemistry student at college, filling his room with bottles, crucibles, test tubes, and retorts. There was no laboratory then, so this had to serve. Probably it was a proof of his skill that North Hall was not blown to bits in some experiment.

If Dr. Carr led John into those subjects which meant most to him, it was to Mrs. Carr he was indebted for even finer insights. Young, alert, and gifted, she was the "little lady of the fair committee," who had seen to it that the young Scotsman won his prize. Now, in her home, the first center of culture that he had ever known, he was given glimpses of a wider world, which it was his destiny to enter. Later, John was to write of its "peace, kindness and patience" and of the beautiful book-lined library, which seemed to him its heart. Here he met the great minds, from Agassiz to Emerson and Thoreau.

As for the small fry who lived here too, it became his duty to take the boys in tow, along with young Henry Butler, almost every Saturday. The "pleasantest way in the world to turn an honest penny," especially as dinner was included.

After commencement in June, 1861, John went home for nine weeks' work on his father's farm. When the end of August came, time for the beginning of the fall term, two boys went back to Madison with money to meet the first tuition bill. John, rejoicing in his powers of persuasion, took Davie with him.

The Madison they found was not the quiet university town John had left. Stores and saloons had mushroomed up. Soldiers were everywhere and all the riffraff came to prey upon them. Here a group of officers came swaggering, with clanking swords, elbowing the "college children" out of the way. It was all confusing, ugly—and exciting.

When John saw a lad from home reeling out of a saloon, plainly unable to handle his load, his conscience was roused. He began to go out to Camp Randall, looking up the men he knew from up Portage way. He marveled at the filth and confusion of the camp, at the boredom and disease. He invited the boys to visit his college room, showed them his experiments, tried to win their confidence. Lonely farm boys, many of them far too young. The Daniel in John was on top now. He urged them "not to go to pieces," to "resist temptation," to remember that "they must live after the war."

In October he went to the station to see the 7th Wisconsin off for the front, men of every nationality—Scotch, German, Irish, Swedish, American Indian. He was deeply troubled as he watched the trains pull away. Going back, he sat down to write a letter to Mrs. Pelton, who was still his friend and confidante.

"I helped Byron buckle on his knapsack. Dwight with his fife seemed uncommonly happy, but oh, what a terrible work is assigned them!"

"A terrible work." Perhaps John Muir, writing that afternoon with deep foreboding in his heart, was gifted with the foresight of the true Scotsman. For the men of the 7th Wisconsin, who went away so gaily that day, were to become part of the famous Iron Brigade. In the bloodiest battles of the war they took their part, from Gainesville to Gettysburg. From the terrible conflict at Cemetery Hill few among them ever came home.

In the mid-term of winter '61 and '62 (there were three terms of thirteen weeks each in the year) John and Davie knocked off studying to teach school: an easy way, they thought, to meet the next tuition bill.

John wrote to Sarah:

The Monday morning that I commenced teaching I did not know where to look, nor what to say, nor what to do. A mud turtle upside down on a velvet sofa was as much at home! I heard a pupil declare that the teacher didn't seem "to know bran," but all moves with ease now.

With great relief John went back to his spring term at college, which ran from March twenty-sixth through the month of June. Good to be back when the fresh life about him was starting its own new term. Good to take his ice-cold dip in Lake Mendota of a morning, or to greet the thrushes in the woods beyond his window!

Though the country round him spoke of fresh, new life, the words on men's lips, the shrieking headlines of the press, bore a sterner message. And always, in these days, sleeping or waking, it seemed to John that he heard the hypnotic beat of drums—drums—drums. Not alone for marching or drill, but now the funeral drum rolled out its muffled, dark rhythm. Camp Randall was in desperate straits in these days of spring, 1862. Men were dying from spoiled and poisonous food, from contagion, pneumonia, dysentery, smallpox, as well as from wounds.

Was the nation dying too? The South was at an impasse, but the North could not seem to win. Should he rush to enlist, as most of the college men were doing? The idealism of the North, the bitter plight of the slaves, the cause of union, did not seem to move him overmuch, but man's sickness and suffering—ah, that was a different story! Now he wanted to be a doctor. If he were not caught by the conscription wheel, he would try to find the funds and study medicine.

At the end of spring, again John went home for nine weeks of farm work, this time to the home of Sarah and David, on that same Fountain Lake Farm to which he had come as a child. But oh, how different it was! Freed from the sense of bondage, he loved the peace of the country, the sure routine, the rhythm of the days. His reward? The sight of a goldfinch looping in the sunlight, or the whippoorwill's strange call at evening.

Back in college at the end of August, John began to work hard at geology and chemistry. Since he elected what he wished and avoided other subjects, he was listed in the catalog as an "irregular gent." More than ever the methods of Dr. Carr roused his interest. For this man who had early come under the influence of Agassiz, like the great Swiss naturalist believed in teaching from nature itself. Despite the objection of the rest of the faculty, he took his students outdoors and made them study from the world around them. He taught them many exciting things and showed them signs of early glacial action, for he had become convinced of the truth of Agassiz's theory —"from the universal ice sheet had come the shape of the land." And he rejoiced that Madison was in glacial country.

In these days John Muir was a leader on the campus, known as an "original," but none the less admired for all that. He was chosen president of one of the debating societies. As he always had "the gift of gab" he filled the post with zeal.

It was the end of May and the campus was beautiful in its fresh green; the air was heady with sweetness. For the life of him, John Muir could not work in these spring days! He was thinking of an escape to the woods, as he looked up into the heart of a great locust tree, alive with bloom. Now he saw another student coming toward him,

that "know-it-all Griswold," whom he usually avoided.
But something in the man's eager look, as he caught sight
of John, made him wait for once.

"See you're studying the locust?"

"Yes, beautiful, isn't it?"

"Do you know what family it belongs to?"

"Heavens no!" said John. "Should I?"

"Taste it," Griswold urged. "Here!" He broke off a
bit of the bloom and held it out. John munched it oblig-
ingly. "What does it remind you of?"

"Well, something like fresh peas from the garden."

"You have it, fellow. It does belong to the pea family."

"But one's a weak, straggling vine, the other a tree."

"Doesn't make any difference—they're related. The
ovules or seeds of the locust are in a pod, or legume, like
those of the pea. Man has nothing to do with the classifi-
cation of plants. The botanist has only to examine them
to learn the harmony of relations."

John Muir looked at the once obnoxious Griswold with
amazement. Suddenly he had been given a vision of the
oneness of nature, nature that gave unity through bound-
less variety. He had always been "gey daft" about flowers
and ferns. Now he had a fresh interest in them. Armed
with a copy of Wood's *Botany*, he and Griswold went
botanizing around all the four lakes of Madison that June.

Commencement time at the end of June, 1863. Wistfully John Muir watched the others as they marched up
to receive their diplomas. No graduation certificate for
him, who was only an "irregular gent." But he still had

dreams of the future, of Ann Arbor and the School of Medicine. For the present he would be off on a botanizing wander with two of his best college friends, down the Wisconsin river gorge and on into Iowa.

Reaching Prairie du Chien after weeks of wandering, he went to call at the Mondell House, where once he had been so happy. He knew that Mrs. Pelton was dead, but he waited eagerly for a glimpse of Emily. When she came to meet him, she seemed sadly changed—thin and sober, her lovely face strained and white. Everything to do for her uncle, she told him. She was "manager, hostess, maid of all work." He longed to take her in his arms and comfort her, but someway he resisted. Not yet, he told himself. He was not ready for wife and home and children. Not yet.

There was no doubt that he cared for Emily. All the vivid and careful records of his trip were to go to her in letters. When the "foot journey" was over, he stopped again at the old hotel. This time Mr. Pelton told him that Emily was not there. Feeling sad and rejected, John turned away. Later he found that Mr. Pelton had lied and that Emily was never told of his coming.

Once more in Madison, he gathered up all the relics of his college days, packed the clocks for shipping, the books, the endless papers. How meaningless they seemed now! On a hill back of North Hall he took one last view of his beloved university, of the campus mellow in the sunlight, of Lake Mendota gleaming through the trees. Here he had been for almost three years, secure and happy, excited over his first steps on the long, long road of learning. Would the way lead on, he wondered, as he hoped it might? Or would the war catch and crush him, as it had crushed so many young and hopeful lives? With eyes strangely misted, he lingered for a moment more—then wandered on.

5

"John Muir, Earth Planet, Universe"

JOHN STOOD RAKING THE KITCHEN GARDEN PLOT AT Fountain Lake Farm one early spring morning in 1864. Suddenly he dropped his tool and stood watching the sky. No . . . yes! Rising from the horizon, a line of dots, V-shaped, purposeful, moved up the arc above him, coming nearer, closer. The speed of a race horse, the speed of light. Never wavering, never losing their sharp formation; now he could see the very beat of their wings.

"Wild geese," he cried, "flying north at last!" There was a sharp stab of joy at his heart, which seemed to match the sure, swift purpose of the birds. Yes, the time had come!

That night he sorted out his small collection. He looked wistfully at his plants, at the herbarium filled with mosses, spleenworts, ferns. Would Sarah keep them safe from the children? He cleaned and oiled his plant press and thrust it first into his knapsack. Extra socks, a comb, various oddments. Paper—a compass. Could he take his beloved botany, Burns, and a small New Testament? Now, while

95

the others were sleeping, he borrowed a bit of food from the kitchen. Oatmeal flakes, tea leaves, a big loaf of bread. He was equipped and ready.

All winter he had been restless, and spring had brought his fever to a high urgency. It had been a blow to him that he could not find money for the Medical School at Ann Arbor. He did not know that letters from faculty and students at Madison had gone there for him, only to come back unclaimed, but he did know that his hope and ambition had been thwarted; that it was hard to keep from feeling bitter and lost.

"Stay on and see whether the draft catches you," David had urged. He had waited, but he had not been drafted. For weeks now he had dreamed of visiting the Great Lakes country, or places farther north, well up in Canada. He would go on a long "wander" alone, free as the air. He would study plants, gather specimens, perhaps discover new ones. The days would be timeless, the nights wonderful under the stars.

Oh, he knew what the neighbors were saying! "That Johnny Muir's twenty-five and he hasn't a job yet. What use were them contraptions after all? Why didn't he farm the land his father give him?" Even his brother Davie had turned on him last week with savage words.

"Why don't you give up those confounded weeds, Johnny—find work here in Portage as I have done? Go back and claim your girl, marry, settle down!"

But now the wild geese had called him. He was free!

Early the next morning he stood at the front door waiting to leave, knapsack on back, a good stout stick cut and ready. For a moment he paused, with lifted head, looked up at the sky, raised his hand as if to test the breeze.

"South wind!" he said.

"Another sign of spring," Sarah answered, "but it still looks like winter."

Quickly he embraced her, gave a warm handshake to David, short, quick hugs to little Annie and George. Then he was off, loping across the land, walking as an Indian walks, with easy stride and feet straight ahead. For a long while Sarah stood watching him go. She saw him stop to take a last look at the little meadow by the lake. He loves each grass and fern, she thought, and every flower. Too bad David couldn't do what he asked—sell it to him and keep it fenced so that no animals could trample it. David only laughed about it. Poor John! She could still see him. As he turned for a last wave, she caught the brilliant copper of his hair, tossed by the wind.

Several hours later, waiting for the train at Pardeeville, John pulled paper out of his knapsack and wrote a few words to Emily.

I am to take the cars in about half an hour. I really do not know where I am going. I feel like Milton's Adam and Eve, "The world was all before them where to choose their place of rest."

Good-by, Johnny.

"The world was all before him." So, simply and without fanfare, he started out on the first of his "long, lonely excursions" botanizing "in glorious freedom" around the Great Lakes and far into the Canadian wilderness. By April he was already wading about in northern swamps, by July he had reached the country north of Toronto, exploring the land from Holland River to the heights of Burlington Bay.

Each day had its own delights; each night its special mood and meaning. "Storms, thunderclouds, winds in the woods were welcomed as friends." Often, with food exhausted, he dropped in at a cabin on some lonely clearing to share for a few brief hours the life that was lived there. Sometimes he went to bed supperless or slept without blankets, but rarely failed to be given "a big, backwoods loaf of bread."

It was late afternoon. For hours John had been forcing his way through a great tamarack and cedar swamp, now climbing over slimy logs, now plunging into deep icy water. He was weary, faint, and discouraged. Though he had set his course by the compass, the twisting route, the constant floundering, had left him dazed. By all his reckoning he should have come out of this place long ago.

Death in life, life in death, he thought, beauty and deformity, as he looked at the tall white cedars with drooping branches that slashed at his face, or saw the rotting logs at his feet. About him lay slimy green water—dark

and someway sinister. Now he saw the ripple of a water snake. In the distance a beaver whined at work.

The shadows lengthened, the light grew dim. The oily green of the water turned black. Must he spend the night in this evil place, with no dry land on which to lay his head?

It was then he saw it. First a clear, rippling stream of water, gushing pure and fresh from the ground, so different from the bog around it. On the further bank a lovely bed of yellow moss stretched like gold, and from its center, showing pure and ghostly in the half-light, gleamed a single exquisite flower.

With a cry of delight, which only the silence heard, John plunged forward. Throwing himself down on the bank, he stretched out reverent hands to the white flower, which grew in its pure beauty from the slime. He needed no botany to tell him what it was, for he knew at once that rare orchid, which few men know and fewer still have found—*Calypso Borealis*, the lonely "Hider of the North."

How long he sat examining his discovery John never knew, but there was still light to guide him when he splashed on. Now he felt "strong, exhilarated, all weariness gone." Soon came a rise of ground, the brown of a log cabin against the green of maple trees. An old Scots woman, clay pipe gleaming faintly in her mouth, came to the door in welcome.

"Where ha' ye come fra? The swamp, that awfu'

swamp? Mony a puir body has been lost in that cauld, dreary bog—and never found. It's God's mercy ye ever got out!"

Days later, remembering Dr. Butler's request for word from him, John decided to write. What better news could he send than his strange story of the white flower? Much moved by the letter, with its descriptive power, the good professor sent it on to an eastern paper, which published it. In the dusty newsprint of the *Boston Recorder* the lonely "Hider of the North" lived again, the first writing of John Muir's ever to appear in print.

John and Danny managed to meet at Niagara Falls. As they camped at the edge of a juniper forest, overlooking the river, they talked till late at night beside their campfire.

"Time to hole up for the winter!" the practical Danny told his oldest brother. "You'd better come back with me to Trouts' Hollow on Lake Huron. Low wages, but good work. The men who run the mill are a fine crew."

"I'm no groundhog—I'd rather stay on top of the earth and go wandering!"

"But not in the snow," said Danny.

In the end, John took Danny's advice. He liked the little mill, set in a wild gorge, liked the whine of the saws and the answering roar of the river. He was childishly amused by the names of the men in charge and wrote his youngest sisters that he had been hired by a "Trout" and a "Jay."

It was a good winter, ushered in by a fine fall. But

with the coming of spring, John's old restlessness returned. Again the V of the wild geese. Blue herons stood statue-like in the river, and the sky was black with migrating birds. In the woods, shy, veined hepaticas and the white trillium appeared as if by magic. John thought wistfully of Emily and wrote to her again, though he had not heard from her.

> Meaford P.O.
> County of Gray
> Canada, W.
>
> My friend Emily:
> I wrote you on the first of last January and have not yet received an answer. . . . Whether this comes from your being sick, or married, or crazy, or angry, I could not decide. . . .

To add to John's spring fever came the blow of Danny's decision to leave. He "needed to earn more money and must look for work in some big city." Knowing that the boy wished to go to college, John could not oppose him.

Bereft without Danny, longing for Emily, made achingly alive by the lonely beauty of the place, John's thought went out to the Madison friends who had been so kind to him. He wrote to Professor Butler and to Henry, his young partner at the fair. In September he sent the first of his letters to Mrs. Carr, who now became the confidante that Mrs. Pelton had tried to be. A woman of culture, gifted in the arts, a trained botanist, friend of many learned and distinguished people, she became perhaps the most formative influence in John Muir's life.

Trout's Mill near Meaford
Sept. 13th, 1865

Dear Mrs. Carr;

Your precious letter with its burden of cheer and good wishes has come to our Hollow. . . . Since undertaking a month or two ago to invent new machinery for our mill, I am so buried in work that I am fit for little else. . . .

I would like to go back to College, but then I have to say to myself, "You will die ere you can do anything else!" I should like to invent useful machinery, but it comes, "You do not wish to spend your lifetime among machines." . . . I should like to practise medicine, but again it comes, "You will die ere you are ready to do so." . . . And oh, how intensely I desire to be a Humboldt!

So Mrs. Carr learned to understand a man of many talents and gifts, torn and troubled by the conflict between them. She sensed the brilliant promise, the keen, sensitive spirit, the fine ambition. More than anyone else she helped to make John Muir a citizen of the world, by giving him her faith and friendship.

All through the long Canadian winter, John stayed in

the Hollow, inventing gadgets to speed up the work of the mill. By spring he would have met a contract for thirty thousand broom handles and twelve thousand rakes. The handles were already finished and stored for seasoning; beside him lay six thousand rakes. He had been promised fifty per cent of the profits. Just a little more work and he would be free to leave, with money in his pocket and a big, fat check in his wallet.

It was late on a cold night in March when John sat stooped over his herbarium. Outside all day a blizzard had been raging. Now the snow had stopped, but the wind still tore at the shutters and wailed round the little cabin. Suddenly John's keen ears caught a new and different sound above the roar of the storm. Quickly he raised his head to listen. What was that curious ripple of light, flickering across his frosted windowpanes? As he gazed at it, with a sleepy curiosity, the whole window turned to a brilliant ruby red.

Quickly he flung up the sash, knowing, even as he hated to know, what would lie below. Across the pond the mill stood a flaring inferno of flame, and all the Hollow was filled with a glaring light that sparkled in the snow. By morning the mill, with all its contents, had burned to the ground. All that was left of John Muir's inventions was a mass of twisted, useless rubble.

John and his brother sat side by side on a sagging cot

in Danny's Buffalo boardinghouse. Over their knees lay stretched a big map and John's lean, brown finger traced a line across it.

"I'll bear off to the left a bit—so," he was saying, "through Ohio, Indiana, and Illinois. I don't think I'll stop till I'm here." His finger tip hid a large, black spot on the map until Danny pushed it aside.

"Indianapolis?"

"Yes."

"Why do you choose it?"

"See all this network of lines about the center? Railroads. That means material shipped in and plenty of manufactured goods shipped out. They must need workers. See this other black spot at the city's edge?"

"Yes—what?"

"It's one of the largest forests in all America."

Only a few hours after John reached Indianapolis, he found a job in the big steam-driven factory of Osgood, Smith and Company, where wagon parts were made. Hubs, spokes, and felloes were turned out by the hundreds amid "the earnest rush, roar and whirl of the machines," strong music which the young inventor loved.

At first he was put in charge of one circular saw at the modest wage of ten dollars a week. By the following week, at almost double the salary, he was made supervisor of all of them. Soon his head was spinning with plans for laborsaving devices and new equipment, a fact not lost to his employers.

John was lonely and wrote to his sister, Sarah. "I never

before felt so utterly homeless as now." But this mood
soon passed. When he was invited by a fellow worker,
Levi Sutherland, a good Scotsman, to come and share his
house, comfortable, and gay with children, he felt settled
at last.

Soon another delightful thing happened. As usual he
had sent his new address to Dr. Butler in Madison, who
responded with a letter of introduction to one of his own
special friends. Miss Catherine Merrill, professor of English literature at Butler University, was, like Mrs. Carr,
a person of influence. She was the second woman in the
United States ever to be offered a college professorship
but, in spite of this stupefying fact, had kept all her sim-
plicity, sense of humor, and charm. She took an instant
liking to the tall young Scotsman who came so diffidently
to her door one Sunday afternoon, and listened enthralled
to the story of his Canadian "wanders." Soon he was
introduced to many of her friends, always welcome in her
special circle, and ended by becoming a kind of Pied Piper,
who took them on nature walks in the forest almost every
Sunday. Both inside and outside the factory, John felt
that he had won a place.

One evening John stayed late in the shop to do a repair
job. He was weary. He had recently put in a counter-
shaft for a new circular saw and had to shorten a belt,
which connected it with the main shaft. The belt, which
was also new, had stretched under strain.

Stooping low to see clearly in the dim lamplight, he
started to unlace some stitches in the belt with a long file,

sharply pointed at the tip. The stitches were fine; the belt resisted. Now, with a twist of the tool, he put more pressure against the leather. Suddenly the file turned in his hand and sprang up against his face, with the sharp end uppermost. He felt a stinging pain in his right eye, pain which changed to a cruel anguish.

Fighting for self-control, John pressed his hands over his face and stumbled toward one of the dimly lighted windows. He struggled to open the eye which hurt so cruelly. Slowly he took away his hands. Was vision left? Would the twilight reassure him? But to his horror it was a world of utter darkness in which he stood and, in that moment of agony, he knew that he was blind.

For days John Muir lay in a darkened room in Levi Sutherland's house. He could not see the faces that stooped over him with compassion. Night and day were the same, a nightmare time of pain, which left him weak and sick. And now came despair. What could he do? What would ever become of him?

The Sutherlands sent for their family doctor, who said that the left eye might recover from its sympathetic nerve shock, the right one—never. Meanwhile he must lie in darkness, for light might injure the little vision left. It was a bitter verdict.

"I am lost," John wrote to his beloved Professor Butler, in a crooked, sprawling handwriting unlike his own. "Lost in the darkness of a terrible valley, which has gashed my life from side to side."

It was Miss Catherine Merrill at last who had the

wisdom to help him. She came, bringing a famous eye specialist to examine him. Though cautious in his verdict, he told John that he would not be blind for life. In time, after weeks of rest, he would be able to see.

"Able to see." So intense was the relief and joy that it was almost too poignant to bear. Now the nightmares rolled away, the dark valley became a mountaintop. This was the future. This was the white flower in the forest—this was hope.

One day while he was still sick his two employers came to call. They told him of a new shop about to be opened, of which he could be foreman, with higher pay and shorter hours. In the near future—a partnership. When they left he promised them an answer soon. This was courtesy, for his mind was made up. In the long hours of darkness he had found the solution for his inner conflict. "God has to almost kill us sometimes to teach us a lesson."

On a fair day in April John went back to the woods for the first time after weeks of illness. The breath of spring greeted him, the warm wind blew a welcome. Yes, thank God, he could still see the lovely pattern of light and shade across the floor of the forest, still see the white of the rue anemone! The world, which he thought he had lost, was here, all about him. With his back against a huge, elephant-gray beech trunk, he dedicated himself to it in full and final surrender.

Never again the rush of factories, the whirr and roar of machines, the confusion and conflict! He would forever desert "the inventions of men and give himself to the inventions of God." Nor would he do this in aimless self-indulgence. This was no child's lark, no idle game.

All his life, he thought, he had wanted to find the relationship between man and nature. Man through the years had been the despoiler of nature, the ruthless conqueror, hostile alike to the earth that spawned him and to his fellow men. But he should find another road. There was a unity which gave pattern to the flower and leaf, or swung the planets about the sun. Could he become part of it, unlock its meaning? He—John Muir—would turn to the wilderness he loved as a humble student, seeking to solve the mystery of life.

On September 1, 1867, John took the train from Indianapolis to the South. In a small rubber bag he had placed a few possessions with three small books: the New Testament, Milton's "Paradise Lost," his beloved Burns. The plant press went into his knapsack. Now he added a notebook, for he meant to keep a record, with sketches, of his long journey. On the fly leaf of the little journal he wrote the lonely, ambitious heading, "John Muir, Earth Planet, Universe," and drew a gay decoration.

At Louisville, Kentucky, John left the train to start out on his great adventure, a thousand-mile walk to the Gulf of Mexico.

I might have become a millionaire, he thought, but instead—I chose to become a tramp.

6

The Range of Light

THE END OF MARCH IN THE YEAR 1868. TWO MEN STOOD on a San Francisco wharf, looking out toward the coastal steamer *Nebraska,* whose dinghy had just landed them. One watched all the life of the bay, while the other gazed across the Golden Gate toward the towering, beautiful peak of Mount Tamalpais.

One man was tall, broad-shouldered, lean, and strong. In spite of dingy jeans, and a frayed and faded coat, he had an air of confidence and self-respect. The other, small, restless, and nondescript, wrapped in a greatcoat many sizes too large, looked as if he had stepped out of a novel by Charles Dickens.

"Well, Chilwell," the tall man said, "shall we be getting on with it?"

"Lead on, Scottie!" the little cockney answered.

John Muir and his shipboard companion wandered along Market Street looking about them. Who in all this rushing crowd could give them the directions they needed? Now a carpenter with his kit of tools.

John stopped him with a word. "Would you be kind enough to tell us the quickest way out of the city?"

"Where do you want to go?"

"Anywhere that's wild," John answered.

The carpenter eyed them narrowly, directed them to the Oakland ferry, then hurried off.

Soon they were wandering out of Oakland, south to the Santa Clara Valley. Then on, out of Gilroy, to the "enchanting Pacheco Pass, which resounded with crystal waters and the loud shouts of thousands of quails." From the height of fifteen hundred feet, they looked down on the central valley of California, stretching north and south as far as the eye could see, "one flower garden, smooth and level as a lake of gold."

But it was not the level plain which made the blood pound faster in John Muir's veins. There, from the eastern side of the valley, rising miles in height, looking like a cloud in the sunny sky, towered the vast wall of the Sierra, the great mountains he had come around the world to see. For them he had deserted the coast of Cuba and given up his dream of exploring South America. Now they stood before him, "so gloriously colored and so luminous, they seemed to be not clothed with light, but wholly made of it."

"The Range of Light!" John cried aloud. "Not the Snowy Range, the Sierra Nevada—that's the wrong name —the Range of Light."

Coming down from the Pacheco Pass, wandering along

the central plain, they came at last to Hills Ferry and crossed the San Joaquin River. John knew that it was the Merced which drained the famous Yosemite he wished to find. Soon they followed along the winding river, up through the foothills to the mining town of Coulterville, where a storekeeper told them to turn back.

"Find the Yosemite? You're crazy! The trails are buried in snow ten feet deep. You'll be lost and helpless. Here's your flour and tea—at least buy a gun."

John stowed away the meager supplies, grudgingly bought an old army musket, then called back over his shoulder as he left, "I never get lost in the wilds!"

"Well, remember I warned you!" the storekeeper shouted back.

John Muir left little record of these days and nights in the Yosemite, of which later he was to be the great interpreter, though for over a month the two men played about, exploring the icy valley like schoolboys on a holiday. At last, thin with hunger, they decided to leave by way of Wawona, Galen Clark's station on the South Fork. For two days they wallowed along a heavy, snow-filled trail, never losing their way, but following a compass and the lay of the land. Clark, the pioneer, welcomed them with amazement, filled their flour sack and gave them a slab of bear meat.

On at last to the Mariposa Grove, where John had his first view of the "greatest and oldest of all living things, the majestic sequoias." Of this, later, he wrote in his journal, "We camped here long, uncounted days, wandering about from tree to tree, taking no thought of time."

The vacation was over. With empty pockets, half starved, the two men returned to the blistering San Joaquin plain. Here the grain was standing high, waiting for the harvest. At Thomas Egleston's ranch Chilwell and John Muir found ready work.

Through these days of his first California spring, John was to run the gamut of many jobs. First, the old familiar one of swinging the scythe. When the harvest was in, Chilwell drifted on and John hired himself out as sheep-shearer with a "mongrel group of men"—Spaniards, Indians, Irish, English, and Scotsmen. They were rough and devil-may-care, but he had no trouble with them.

The next job was more to his taste. Wild horses, heritage of the Spaniards, still roamed the California plains in these days of 1868. It was catch-as-catch-can and a lively prize for any man who could rope them! Now John went back to the Egleston ranch to break in broncos. By a mixture of gentleness, firmness, and understanding he slowly tamed them, never by cruelty. As he sat one of the bucking little beasts, which was trying hard to unseat him, he often thought of his pony Jock. Again he wondered what had ever become of him.

John Muir's first job in the fall was with Pat Delaney, a tall, charming Irishman, who at once gained his liking. He had been educated for the priesthood, lured away by California gold, and now had settled down on his own ranch near La Grange. Before John left him, the two men were warm friends.

Sheepshearing again, with its quick and ready profit; then the offer of a winter job tending a herd, which belonged to Smoky Jack, one of the big sheep men of the district. A young shepherd up Rocky Creek was quitting, he told John. He must find a good man at once. "Thirty dollars a month and board—a foin, aisy job."

John, knowing little of sheep and liking them even less, tried to escape from this, but Smoky Jack was firm. "Just follow the road between French Bar and Snelling four or five miles. When you see a cabin on a little hill, that's the place. Sure, 'twill all go smooth and aisy."

In December John walked out to claim his flock. After all, he did need a job! Yes, he found the place, and a queer, dismal enough spot it proved to be, a dingy cabin with a broken roof and a yard full of filth. The young shepherd greeted him with joy, slung a bundle over his shoulder, and started to run. In vain John begged him to "spend the night and show him the range."

"Not a bit of use," the boy answered. "Sheep'll show it to you. All you have to do is just open the corral in the morning and run after them like a coyote all day. Yep! They'll show you the range." With a wave of his hand the youngster rushed away.

Pretty grim, John thought, as he looked at the filthy cabin. A Dutch oven, a few tin cups, a black frying pan, caked with grease, lay on the floor, plus one wooden water bucket. There was a sort of rickety shelf in one corner. Perhaps meant for a bed? John thought he'd rather sleep on the ground outside. But here he had noted filth and ashes indescribable, with old shoes, rams' horns, old jaws and craniums. Besides all that, some prowling, vicious-looking wild hogs.

He lay down on the hard bed shelf and stretched himself out with a sigh. Well, enough was enough! He could leave tomorrow as the young shepherd had done. Then, seeing the stars gazing down through the broken roof, he forgot his woes and drifted into sleep.

The next day, when he let down the bars of the corral, the whole flock came crowding out, bleating and baaing like water "escaping from a broken flume." They crossed Dry Creek and scattered over a dozen hills. When he drove them back toward the cabin at sunset time, to his great surprise the sheep formed themselves into long parallel lines and marched into the corral.

For eight months John Muir lived in this lonely spot, but he soon learned to be content. Sensitive to every change of nature, he watched with joy the coming of the spring rains, turning the dark, drought-stricken land to living green. Mosses appeared, tall waving ferns, charming beds of violets, clover, tulips, and mints. Now the sheep grew sleek and manageable, as they filled themselves with good green grass. This was a botanist's paradise!

At night he painted in his journal vivid word pictures of each day's discovery. "The nearest foothills are now

rosy purple. . . . Beyond and above all, the summit peaks are pure, deep white."

"March fourteenth. Killed a rattlesnake that was sunning himself in coiled ease about a bunch of grass. . . . I killed him by jumping on him, because no stones or sticks were near. He defended himself bravely and I ought to have been bitten. He was innocent and deserved life."

The months passed till by early June the plains country had become a burning oven, from which John longed to escape. The dream of the mountains was always with him. He must—he knew he would—somehow, soon, manage to go back to the cool, life-giving forests.

Strange that at this moment Pat Delaney should happen by to ask his help. The tall Irishman, whom John had nicknamed Don Quixote, spoke firmly. "Muir, will you do something for me? My sheep are starving, since every green thing has gone. Will you drive them up to the mountains and ride herd on them this summer? Surely, you don't wish to stay in this burning hell?"

A door opening, a leap of joy at his heart! John spoke impulsively. "Yes, anywhere in the Sierra!" Then he added slowly, "But perhaps I shouldn't. I don't know much about the ways of sheep in the mountains. They might fall into canyons, be eaten by bears, drown in rivers, be caught in thorny chaparral—I've had no experience."

The Don laughed and clapped him on the shoulder. "What a list of horrors! True, any one of them might happen. But the hard work is not to be yours. I'll send a shepherd along to do the herding, with two or three men to help him. You can roam about, climb and study at will. I'll pay you a salary. But you'll be there in an emergency and you're to see that the men keep on the job. I'll go along in the beginning."

Sunrise time on the French Bar ranch, near the Tuolumne River. Already the air was stifling. John's back was wet with sweat as he helped to stow away pans, kettles, blankets, bundles of clothes, and bags of food on the restless pack horses. Then he added his plant press to one saddlebag.

The pack horses were ready. The corral gate was opened and the sheep plunged out, bleating and coughing in a cloud of dust. Delaney, musket on shoulder, led the march with the horses; Bill, the shepherd, with his Chinese helper, prodded one flank. On the other, an Indian, calm, impassive, kept the sheep in line. John himself came on behind, singing Scottish ballads at the top of his lungs. "Scots Wha Hae wi' Wallace Bled" was a fine marching tune. So the "great, gray blanket" rolled over the land and up through the foothills.

It was slow going, for heat made the sheep listless. At noon, the glare of the sun seemed unbearable; then the air began to grow fresher. Was there a breath of wind from the Sierra, a lift, a faint scent of pine? The leaders pressed forward, as if some lost memory of mountain pastures had returned to them. A thrill seemed to run through the entire flock, which moved forward faster, eager and united.

On and on, always upward toward the mountains! The first permanent camp was made on a branch of the north fork of the Merced, at the foot of Pilot Peak ridge. Tall trees shaded the campsite. At three thousand feet the worst of the heat had vanished. At the foot of tumbling rapids in the stream stretched lily beds with orange and purple flowers, on stems six feet tall. Joy filled John Muir's heart when he found them. In his journal he called them "children of light."

But soon, as the weeks passed, all the beautiful land within a radius of two miles of the camp was trampled and devoured. How John hated the foraging sheep! Not for themselves, poor silly things, but for the harm they caused. He called them "hoofed locusts" and wished to drive them from the wilderness.

The pasturage was exhausted; even the shepherds' food was scarce, when Delaney returned to guide them to a new spot. Now the snows would be melted from upper meadows. They could make a camp above the Great Wall.

On their way they stopped at Tamarack Flat, only five miles from the lower end of the Yosemite. An icy brook rushed bank high through a lush meadow, but John noticed that just below their camping place, the ground was bare gray granite, strewn with rocks. This was a strange contrast. With curiosity he rushed down to investigate.

Then he saw that many of the huge boulders were different in color and composition from the granite around them. How had they gotten here? What mysterious force had quarried and lifted and laid them down, each in its place? For a long time he bent over the granite pavement, looking in the glare of the sun for revealing marks. And then he knew, or thought he knew, the answer.

For the man who had listened to Ezra Carr at Madison and learned, fascinated, the theories of Agassiz, jumped to a quick conclusion. That night he noted down with care: "The most resisting part of the surface is scored and striated in a rigidly parallel way, indicating that the region has been overswept by a glacier from the northeastward, grinding down the general mass of the mountains, scoring and polishing, producing a strange, raw, wiped appearance, and dropping whatever boulders it chanced to be carrying at the time it was melted, at the end of the Glacial Period."

Then John Muir added with a flourish, "A fine discovery—this!"

A fine discovery! That night he had no faintest premonition that this leap of intuition, still to be confirmed by long and careful search, was to loose an angry argument which would rock the world of science from end to end.

By midsummer John Muir was a real mountaineer. Pathless forests, wild and tortuous canyons, windswept peaks seemed to call to him; the darkness was his friend. Delaney, on one of his rare visits to help move the herd, was amazed at the speed with which John covered the rough trails. He was hard put to it to keep up with him.

Now he looked at this hired hand with amazement, as they sat on a great shoulder of rock for what John called "a blink of rest." In his dark, hobnailed shoes and rough gray clothes he seemed not unlike the granite beneath him. Only the keen, humorous eyes, almost too blue in the weathered brown face, and the bright green pine tip in his buttonhole revealed the artist, the man of parts.

"Muir."

"Aye."

"You say you were born on the north coast of Scotland. You came to America at eleven, to the hill country of Wisconsin."

"Aye."

"How do you account for the fact that you're a mountain climber?"

"Some strange alchemy of the blood, I suppose!" Then John laughed. "Perhaps it was the scootchers of my childhood."

"The what?"

"Oh, tests of courage and daring my brothers and I went in for. We were always hell-bent on catching each other out."

"Such as?"

"Hanging from window ledges or walking the rooftree at night or scrambling like goats along the walls of Dunbar Castle or down into rotting old dungeons."

"How could that explain you?"

"Not bad training for a mountain climber."

It was a day in July when John Muir had been following the Mono trail. Now he buckled back to the west
side of Indian Canyon, then traced the Valley rim to the
west. He was searching for spots on the very brink, where
he could look down the face of the wall to the bottom.
Three thousand feet straight down! At first this made
him dizzy and sick. Each time, as he crawled back, his
mind said to his body, "Don't go out on the verge again."
Each time his body disobeyed him. Under the spell of
Yosemite, the mind seemed to have no power of its own.

At last he pressed on, looking for the spot where Yosemite Creek pours its shining flood over the edge of the
terrible cliff, half a mile of snowy foam, down, down,
down to the world below. Taking off his shoes and
socks, he worked his way along the rushing stream, keeping his feet and hands pressed firmly on the polished
rock. This gave him traction and self-confidence. Now
at the edge of the great leap, could he lean far out and
watch the "form and behavior of the fall" all the way
to the bottom?

No, again he was disappointed. There was a brow of
rock, over which he could not see, too steep and slippery
for human feet. Then, far below, he saw a narrow ledge
about three inches wide on the very brink, just wide
enough for a pair of heels.

Made giddy by the roaring of the water, above, below, and beside him, he decided not to try to reach this
ledge. One hand clutched at a tuft of artemisia, growing

in a crevice of the rock. As he chewed the bitter leaves, his head cleared.

Though he had decided not to venture, his body slid downward. He reached the ledge, moved slowly along it to the very edge of the roaring mass of water and had a perfectly free view down into the heart of the great falls. Drenched with spray, still clinging desperately to the cliff behind him, he felt exhilarated and unafraid, all terror destroyed by the "grandeur of form and sound and motion."

How long he stayed, or how he managed to climb back, he could never remember. By darkness he arrived at camp, weary and footsore, but triumphant.

In September John led the flock down to their home ranch on the plain. He went with many a backward look at the mountains. He had had a wonderful summer, sketching, climbing, hiking, and studying. Not books, but the living things about him. The mountains were in his blood now; he was part of them. The lonely, windswept peaks, the lovely alpine meadows, plunging white waters, dim, cool magnificent forests.

"I have crossed the Range of Light," he wrote, "surely the brightest and best of all the Lord has built and, rejoicing in its glory, I gladly, gratefully, hopefully, pray I may see it again."

7

Rivers of Ice

FOR SEVERAL WEEKS JOHN STAYED AT DELANEY'S RANCH below French Bar, but he was restless, pulled by one desire. Taking Harry Randall, a tenderfoot from the East, along with him, he started back to the Yosemite.

John and Harry sat by their campfire in the Valley, watching the sparks rocket up into darkness. The roar of Yosemite Falls was in their ears. They could dimly see the lights of the upper hotel, which stood on the bank of the Merced, facing the great cascade. A hotel in this wilderness? It seemed to John a sacrilege.

As they drank their scalding tea and chatted in low tones, suddenly a man slipped into the circle of light and stared down at them. He was tall and spare, with a shock of white hair and a white beard. A long, thick overcoat kept off the November chill. A cultivated, very English voice asked, "Is either of you men John Muir?"

"I am, sir!" John answered without rising.

"Ah! Pat Delaney has spoken of you. You were here in

the summer with his herds? Do you know anything about carpentry—or running a mill?"

"May I ask to whom . . ." John sprang up and waited.

"Oh, yes, I'm Hutchings, owner of the hotel. I've built a mill, but there's something wrong with it. I need a sawyer—better still, a good mechanic. I've cottages to raise, new partitions for the hotel. We've used curtains for rooms long enough."

"It happens that I am a millwright, Mr. Hutchings, but . . ."

"Why, that's marvelous, stupendous! Will you come to look things over tomorrow, tell me what's wrong?"

"But," John went on, as if he had not been interrupted, "I've promised myself never to cut new timber again."

"This is fallen timber," Hutchings cried eagerly. "Yellow pine, downed in the big blow of '67. I don't cut trees, either. I'm on your side there!" He put out a hand and seized John's firmly.

"Would you have any work for my friend?"

"Well, I need a man to milk cows, drive oxen, haul the logs to the mill."

"But I don't know . . ." young Harry started to splutter, as John's foot, hidden by darkness, moved quickly sideways and caught him on the shin.

"But I'd like to try it!" he ended up tamely.

The next day John told Mr. Hutchings that the water wheel and machinery would have to be made all over again. He was engaged for the work at ninety dollars a month plus board. Harry made himself useful as chore boy for the hotel, learning to milk Buttercup and drive the oxen, Paddy and Duke.

First of all, the two men built themselves a cabin of sugar-pine shakes near the foot of Yosemite Falls, not far from the Hutchings' winter cottage, where they boarded. They were proud of it and John boasted that it was the handsomest house in the Valley. The floor was of slabs from the stream, with cracks left between, through which the ferns could grow; a bit of the stream itself, channeled through a ditch, was brought into the cabin, where John could hear the water rippling and singing on its way. The only window faced the cliff, and the men could watch from their hammocks the sweeping white of the falls at night.

In the long evenings, they leaned back in their heavy, homemade chairs, softened with sheepskins. Sometimes John read aloud or worked on his plant collection, while the rush and roar of water, the wild wailing of winter wind only served to make them feel secure. Letters were few, newspapers nonexistent. Every thirty days Indian Tom came into the Valley on snowshoes, bringing whatever mail the month collected. This was Yosemite in the winter of 1869—lonely, remote—accessible only by steep trails, deep in ice and snow.

The year when he was thirty-one, when he was head herdsman for Pat Delaney's sheep, was an important time for John Muir. Two decisive things happened. First, he had made his fine discovery that there were signs of glacial action in the Yosemite. Second, his beloved friends, the Carrs, moved from Madison to the University of California. They were living in Oakland, and again their home was a center for writers, scientists, teachers, and artists of both West and East.

Through the years Mrs. Carr had never lost interest in the young genius she had discovered at the Madison State Fair, in the student who had so often visited her home. A growing series of letters passed between them. The hunger of youth met by the understanding of maturity.

She shared his love of nature, his passion for plant collecting and study. She understood something of the moods that moved him, his need for loneliness, his hunger for freedom. "John Muir's daemon," she called it, this compulsion under which he acted. But she was afraid for him that he might become too isolated, even queer in his hermit ways. She wanted him to know other men who would share his interests and appreciate his gifts. One thing she could do for him. She had made up her mind to this! In the spring, when famous friends of theirs left for the Yosemite they went carefully briefed, or with letters in their pockets for "our promising student, John Muir."

With his discovery of glacial action and his quick conclusion that rivers of ice had formed and moulded the vast canyons of the Sierra, John's life found a new dimension. Now he was a man with a mission—to prove, to himself at least, that his theory was right and to find the evidence. Not that he thought then of a reputation to be earned, fame to be achieved. Not at all. A fact must be proved or disproved, for one's own satisfaction. Could it be that in some lofty valley a lost glacier might still be lingering, that the hand of ice might still be writing the future?

The work of the mill was constant and hard. There were partitions to be built in the hotel, new cottages to be started, all to be done before Hutchings returned in the spring. For the master of the house was in Washington, trying to defend his claim to land which he had bought in 1864, the upper hotel and one hundred and sixty acres, when the Yosemite was still in the public domain.

In a sense Hutchings had been "hoist by his own petard." A San Francisco editor, he had been the first to rouse the nation's interest in this "scenic wonder" by his writing in the *Mariposa Gazette*. Through a wave of public pressure, Congress was persuaded to pass a bill, saying that "the cleft or gorge known as Yosemite with the Mariposa Grove of great sequoias, shall be held for public use." It was signed by Lincoln at the end of the war and became the first wilderness park of the United States. In 1866 California accepted the grant "for public use, resort and recreation." But in so doing, she gave no legal status to early landholders. So Hutchings was forced to a long fight for his rights.

By the middle of April John discovered that a new chore had been given him. Now on foot, mule, or horseback the curious tourists began to arrive. To John fell the dubious pleasure of showing them the sights. How he raged inwardly at hearing Yosemite Falls called "pretty" or magnificent Half Dome "charming!"

When Hutchings returned in May, John felt a new tension in the air. Had the Englishman been soured by his struggle with Washington? Was he jealous because his little girl tagged John and ignored her father? Perhaps, because he himself was used to playing center stage, to posing as the great authority on Yosemite, he disliked the fact that visitors questioned John, as if he had some mine of information.

Jealous, resentful, even hostile. With his usual intuition, Muir knew that he was out of favor. So it was no surprise when Hutchings told him to "get back in the mill and stay there," that he would "be needed as a guide no longer." And to John it was relief, rather than punishment. But his exile was short-lived. Hutchings was well aware of Dr. and Mrs. Carr's influence and distinction. When friends of theirs arrived, carrying letters to John Muir or asking where he might be found, he was wise enough to recall his handyman. Now Mrs. Carr's little plot was working itself out. During the next two years a stream of famous guests, impressive enough to fill a small *Who's Who* would come to Yosemite and ask to meet John Muir.

It was a joy when word came that Joseph LeConte, teacher of geology at the University of California, was to visit the Valley. Yet there was a disturbing element in it too. For here, John knew, was a distinguished scientist who, by his disapproval, might brand as nonsense this new discovery of his, might shake even his own belief in it. And yet, if he could convince LeConte, could make him see that glacial action had helped to form the Yosemite, what wings would be given to his own faith, what meaning to the future!

So far, whenever he had spoken of his findings to interested guests, he had met only stares or disbelieving headshakes. "But—Whitney . . ." was the answer.

Whitney was the famous Harvard teacher, now the official geologist of California. He had made a careful survey of the Coast range and the Sierra. John had read the first volume of his study, published in 1865, and knew from one end to the other his "Official Guide Book to the Yosemite," brought out the previous year. This was the last word for tourists.

True, in the survey, Whitney's assistant, Clarence King, had mentioned finding glacial marks in the granite, but he had shown no knowledge of their meaning. In the new guidebook, Whitney had "slapped down" his young assistant and called him "in error." "There is no reason to suppose, or at least no proof, that glaciers have ever occupied the Valley, or any portion of it . . . This theory, based on entire ignorance, may be dropped without wasting any more time upon it."

How had the Yosemite been formed—that vast, magnificent Valley? Every tourist wanted to know the answer.

"By an event unique in history," Whitney explained. "By a primal cataclysm, a great catastrophe." In simpler language, "The bottom of the Valley sank down to an unknown depth owing to its support being withdrawn from underneath."

But as far back as early spring, April 13th of that year, John had written to Mrs. Carr, "Whitney says that the bottom has fallen out of the rocks here, which I most devoutly disbelieve."

Presumptuous? Perhaps! Impossible to prove? Well, he would wait to see.

It was midsummer when LeConte came with a group of his university students. Jog-jog-jog, slowly the riding school horses zigzagged along the trail, carrying the boys in their new uniforms, equipped with every kind of weapon from knives to pistols and led by their instructor from West Point.

John could not repress a smile as he noticed the tense and cautious efforts to maintain good form, while, with reins loose on their horses' necks, on hotel mustangs used to rough and slippery trails, he and LeConte rode along easily. The pale, gaunt scientist kept his seat like a veteran. Now and then John twisted in the saddle to point out some distant peak, glacial striations in the granite walls, or the deep, revealing U-shape of the Valley.

The first night they camped under towering fir trees, close to the top of Three Brothers Mountain. As they sat by the fire, LeConte turned to Muir and asked, "I suppose, Mr. Muir, you happen to know that Whitney has heard of your glacial theory?"

"But how?"

"Through returning tourists. There have even been interviews with some of them in the papers. Your name has been publicized, John Muir."

As if caught off guard, John was silent, but looked questioningly at the man beside him. Hesitating slightly, LeConte continued, "He has called you 'only an ignorant sheepherder.' "

For a moment John looked solemn, then his mood changed. Slapping his thigh, he broke into a merry laugh.

"Sheepherder? That's correct, at least! But name calling can't hold a candle to fact finding, can it, Mr. LeConte? As the Scots say, sic a muckle dool—what a peck of trouble. I'll have the facts and even Whitney can't dispose of those."

The second night they camped at the western end of Lake Tenaya, a place which John had visited the year before. Walking along the north shore of the icy blue water, they climbed the great mountain rock at the east end of the lake, burnished and brilliant in the late afternoon sun. John pointed out to LeConte how almost every yard of its surface showed the scoring and polishing action of a glacier, which swept over it from the east, though it was two thousand feet above the lake and ten thousand above sea level.

The third night the party camped on gentian-filled meadows of South Tuolumne, by Soda Springs, a spot later to be important in the career of John Muir. But it was their climb to the red-brown top of Mount Dana two

mornings later, which gave John his chance to show Le-Conte the entire Merced-Tuolumne system, to reveal how two great glaciers must have swept down the Tenaya and Merced canyons, joining in one main river of ice which engulfed the Yosemite, "a mighty cavity, grooved and wrought out for millions of years."

Quietly the older man listened to John's eager explanation. Then, in silence, he studied the sloping shelves of granite, caught below in a wilderness of firs, the mysterious valleys, the peaks lifting themselves against the sky and the faraway, incredibly distant land of blue mist and sunshine in the world beneath.

Later the party wandered on through Bloody Canyon, down to Lake Mono, that strange land of burned-out volcanoes and lost dreams of gold. From here LeConte and his group were to ride to Lake Tahoe, but John felt he must return.

As he started to turn back, LeConte came to him and shook him warmly by the hand.

"We need more evidence," he said, "though what you have shown me is convincing enough. Did I tell you that I was a pupil of Agassiz and helped him in his study of the Florida reefs? Ears to the deaf and eyes to the blind, these you have been to me through this entire week. I admit it freely. I shall go back to tell my university that I accept your discovery. Good-by, and good hunting, John Muir!"

After his trip with LeConte, everything else seemed

insignificant. Now, with the first important approval of his glacial theory to urge him on, he needed to make more observations, to find the final proofs.

It was in 1870 that John Muir thus began to oppose the views of Josiah Whitney.

8

The Golden Eagle

THAT FALL THE RANCH COULD NOT HOLD JOHN MUIR. HE could not be untrue to his central purpose. He must still prove the truth of his glacial theory; also, in a far deeper sense, he belonged to the mountains.

"I will follow my instincts, be myself for good or ill and see what will be the upshot. As long as I live, I'll hear waterfalls and birds and winds sing. I'll interpret the rocks, learn the language of flood, storm, and avalanche. I'll acquaint myself with the glaciers and wild gardens and get as near the heart of the world as I can."

When Hutchings wrote to him in December, asking him to run the mill again, John went back to the Valley. He returned, even though he learned that his cabin was already given to Hutchings' sister. Nothing daunted, he built himself a "hang-nest" under the gable of the mill. From the outside it looked like an unsupported box, which might fall any minute, but it was safe and snug, with a full view of the great falls and a series of planks leading up to it from the mill floor. "The people I dislike are afraid to walk the plank," he wrote to Sarah.

As spring progressed, whenever he could escape from the mill, John went on with his studies, to map out still more clearly the path of ancient glaciers, to note the moraines (that mass of stones and accumulated matter always carried along with them and left behind as they melted) to study the rocks and marks on them, to visit distant, almost inaccessible valleys, hoping, always hoping, to find a lost, living glacier.

In his notebooks he wrote down heights and widths and general findings, or added his own wistful hope of what might yet be found.

"The forces that shaped the mountains, grinding out canyons and lake-like basins, sharpening peaks and crests, bringing domes into relief from the enclosing rocks, carving their plain flanks into their present forms, may yet be seen at work in the High Sierra."

Hope—or prophecy? As yet he did not know.

Early May and tourists were flocking into the Valley. John could not help wondering what new visitor might look him up. Then one day he heard the rumor, running through the hotel crowds like fire through prairie grass, "Emerson is here." "Mr. Emerson, the great writer." "Have you seen Mr. Emerson?"

John was surprised at his own sense of excitement. The years seemed to vanish, and he saw a lanky boy, with legs stretched over one arm of a chair, reading, reading in Dr.

Carr's library, reading "Nature." Reading the poetry which his Scot's heart loved.

> The shadows shake on the rock behind,
> And the countless leaves of the pine are strings
> Tuned to the lay the wood-God sings.

At the end of work that afternoon, he brushed carefully for once what had been called his "glorious auburn hair," changed into a clean, gray shirt, and tucked a pine tip into his buttonhole. Then with the Indian walk that was swift as a run, he went to Leidig's hotel.

Yes, he found the famous Emerson, clad in a greatcoat, though the night was warm, surrounded by his own party of Brahmins from the East. Around the inner circle a changing and widening throng of tourists gaped and listened.

Yes, he saw the fine head, set on shoulders that seemed to stoop with fatigue, saw the blue eyes with their look of detachment and peace, heard the voice which had thrilled so many hearers, which still had resonance and power.

But a strange shyness seized him. Again he was the awkward boy from the back country. At last he rushed away, angry at his own stupidity. The next day, hearing that Emerson was about to leave, he dashed back to the hotel and left a note with the cashier.

Dear Mr. Emerson;
    The mountains wish you to stay longer. El Capitan

and Tissiack demand that you stay longer. . . .

After a few more phrases, he signed himself simply John Muir.

John was at work in the mill. In spite of the whining saw and roaring water, his ears caught a sharp rat-a-tat-tat on the mill door. Quickly throwing it wide, he found Mr. Thayer, leader of the Boston group, standing with up-raised riding crop. Beyond him, on a pied mustang, sat Emerson himself.

"Will you come and speak to Mr. Emerson? He is an-swering your letter in person."

"Nonsense, Thayer! Help me dismount, now that we have found Mr. Muir at home." Somewhat stiffly, Emer-son slipped from the saddle and came forward. "You should have spoken to me the other night, not sent a letter. Any friend of Ezra Carr's . . ."

Though Thayer protested, Emerson climbed the steep slope to the hang-nest, where he examined the herbarium; the drying plants, many of them rare, unclassified speci-mens; all the pencil sketches of mountain peaks, giant trees, or flowers; samples of glacial rocks; notebooks and careful maps, which John kept in his collection. The younger man's shyness ebbed away before the eager curi-osity, the simple, understanding presence of the famous leader.

John was aware of his own copy of Emerson, lying on a cluttered table, the little rust-brown book, the color of a thrasher's back, Volume I of a new edition, which he had bought the year before. His first impulse was to snatch it up and ask the great man to autograph it, but just in time he remembered the scoring and underscoring, which he himself had written in. He had read it from cover to cover, of course, and in some places, on the margin, he had been both rude and brash. "Too strong, Ralph!" he had written in one place. Many sections he had marked with love and appreciation, but—no—the visitor must not see the book! Quickly he drew some papers across it.

Over and over in the following days Emerson came to visit the naturalist and student of the wilderness, as long before he had walked with Thoreau, the wise handyman of Concord. A great affection, a deep sharing of interests grew up between the two men. When the time came for the Boston group to leave the Valley, John was asked to ride with them to the great sequoias in the Mariposa Grove.

"I'll go with your party," John answered, "if you'll camp out with me, Mr. Emerson, under the trees. I'll build an enormous campfire to light up the giants. The night will be glorious!"

"Yes, yes, we must camp out, camp out . . ." Emerson answered, with his radiant smile, but there was a vagueness about his manner which should have warned John Muir.

As they rode along next day through the Sierra forests, Emerson reined his horse in beside John's and questioned him about the different trees. Silver fir, Douglas spruce, libocedrus, or sugar pine, filled the great man with a vast delight.

When they reached Clark's station, John was amazed to find the group dismounting and making ready to stay in the caretaker's tavern.

"But we are camping out!" he cried in dismay.

"Oh, no, Mr. Muir," Thayer answered firmly. "Would you expose Mr. Emerson to the dangerous night air? He might catch cold—he is no longer young."

"Not a cough or a sneeze in the whole Sierra," John protested hotly. "No colds are found under the California sky, only in stuffy hotels and dusty pillows."

But the pliant old man was wax in the hands of his friends, sheltered, left no initiative of his own.

The next day the Thayers, Hathaways, and others chattered their way through the solitude of the sequoias, never coming under their spell. Only Emerson, as his eyes followed the line of a magnificent trunk up, incredibly far up, to the beautiful plumed top, kept a reverent silence. Once he turned to John and said, "There were giants in those days."

Just as the girth straps were being tightened, the pack mules loaded, John made a last desperate appeal. "You are yourself a sequoia," he said. "Stop and get acquainted with your great brothers!"

"My friends will not let me!" Emerson answered, looking like a troubled child.

The party mounted and rode away, winding through

dogwood bushes, in and out between the trunks, up the slope to the edge of the basin, over the divide. Swiftly John followed them. Emerson, who had stayed in the rear, reined in his horse at the top of the ridge, turned in his saddle, and waved farewell.

With a strange sense of loss, Muir returned to the heart of the sequoia grove. He felt that he had never before been lonely in this country, but this time he was lonely. Lonely for the Emerson, prophet of nature, who might have sung these mountains, who would never write or sing of them now. "It was the afternoon of his life and his course was westward, down all the mountains into the sunset."

Troubled, John eased his own hurt, as always, in action. He made a bed of sequoia plumes and ferns by the side of a clear, amber stream, collected his firewood, walked about until darkness came. All the wild things, which had retreated from the chatterers, came out to keep him company. The thrushes with their cool music, the Steller's jays, the Douglas squirrels. At the edge of the forest a doe glanced out and passed with two fawns.

Now a great fire brought the towering trees into bold relief, called out the shadows. But this was Emerson's fire, John remembered. Then the fire died down; the wilderness moved closer. Darkness—and through the high, wind-tossed branches, shone the glory of the stars.

John Muir never saw Emerson again, though letters and gifts went back and forth between them, books from Emerson, a box of cedar sprays from Muir. Emerson wrote, urging him to come to the Atlantic coast, to visit Concord, saying that there were "drawbacks in solitude." After the great leader's death, John Burroughs, looking over a pile of Emerson's papers, found a significant list, with the title, "My Men." It was brief. Carlyle was the name at the top. At the bottom stood John Muir.

After Emerson left, at first the world seemed empty; then John returned to his explorations. For a long time he had felt that a certain canyon in the top of the Valley wall, near the upper falls, must have been chiseled out by a glacier. One morning, with a queer intuition that the time was *now*, he ran up the mountain to the top of the falls, felt the cold spray in his face, and hurried northward full of faith that "there was a writing for him somewhere on the rock."

Four miles further he discovered a narrow hollow where the ice had been compelled to wedge through under great pressure, deeply grooving and hardening the granite. But this was not enough. Still climbing, he followed Yosemite Creek up to its source in the snows of Mt. Hoffman. Here he found all the signs that a living glacier had held this spot, plainly shown by the moraines, masses of boulders and rubble carried by flowing ice and left behind when it melted. *A dead glacier*. Yes, he could even estimate its size—twelve miles long and five wide, though the depth he had no means to measure.

Now came the time when John made a real break for freedom. Long resentful of Hutchings' attitude toward him, he packed up his things and moved to Black's Hotel

down the Valley near Sentinel Rock. Though he did not like interruptions, he was glad to be called on by a new visitor—Merriam of the Smithsonian in Washington, who asked for a complete report of his glacial findings. Now he began to dream of a future free from disturbing jobs.

"I suppose I might live for one or two seasons without work," he wrote to Mrs. Carr. "I have five hundred dollars here and have been sending home money to my brothers and sisters. Some of my friends are begging me to write for the magazines. What do you think about it?"

It was no doubt Muir's last visitor, John Runkle, president of the Massachusetts Institute of Technology, who helped to turn his thoughts toward writing. For five days they hiked through the canyons and over the mountain passes. In the end, Runkle, sure that John's glacial theory was right, asked him to outline it for the Boston Academy of Science. He also begged John to come and teach in his Boston Institute, but the man of the mountains was firm.

"Runkle wants to make a teacher of me, but I have been too long wild to burn well in their high-heated educational furnaces!" The answer was *never*.

In September, true to his promise, John began a series of letters to Merriam and Runkle. Then he sent the same material to the *New York Tribune*. "The Death of a Glacier" was published in December, under another title. To John's amazement, it was paid for in good, hard cash and he was asked for more—the final reward for a canny Scotsman.

A day in October, one of the golden days of Indian summer. Again John was pursuing his eager quest to find, not a dead glacier, but the reality for which he hoped and dreamed—a living glacier still in action in the Sierra.

He was exploring between Black and Red Mountains, two of the peaks of the Merced group, the highest part of a spur that straggles out from the main axis of the range toward Yosemite Valley. Magnificent glacial country, he thought, knowing that the river of ice must have formed and moulded it.

He chose a camping ground on the edge of one of the lakes, where a thicket of hemlock-spruce sheltered him from the wind. The mighty rock walls of the mountains seemed to come nearer, while the starry sky stretched like a ceiling from wall to wall.

Early next morning he set out to trace the grand old glacier that had done so much for the beauty of the Yosemite region. The voices of the mountains were still asleep; no wind stirred the pine needles. The sun was up, but it was still too cold for the birds. Only the stream, cascading from pool to pool, seemed to be wholly awake.

Passing around the north shore of his camp lake, he followed the central stream past many cascades, from lake to lake. The scenery became more rigidly arctic, the dwarf pines and hemlocks disappeared and the stream was bordered with icicles. As the sun rose, rocks were loosened on shattered portions of the cliffs and came down in rattling avalanches.

Tracing the stream back to the last of its chain of lakes,

John noticed a deposit of fine gray silt on its bottom. As it came gurgling out of a raw moraine, he at once suspected that this was glacial mud. Glacial mud! A long-hoped-for clue! The great moraine, one hundred feet high, plunged forward at an angle of thirty-eight degrees. John picked his way slowly up, and there from the top he saw—wonder of wonders—a small, but clearly marked glacier, sweeping down from the precipice of Black Mountain to the very spot on which he stood. *A living glacier*, still in action—proof of all his daring dreams!

The ice showed plainly on the lower section, though gray with dirt and stones, but disappeared further up under coarse snow. Where, in turn, the snow field joined the mountain, stood a deep crevasse, or "bergschrund," fourteen feet wide, bridged here and there by falling avalanches of snow. The bergschrund—how often Dr. Carr had described it to his classes!

With the excitement of a discoverer, John crept along the edge of this deep fissure, clinging to it with numbed fingers. Yes, there were zigzags leading down into its weird underworld of ice. At last he reached the center of the deep glacial hollow, a blue room, hung with icicles and pulsing with a strange, dim light. Overhead, water dripped and murmured and, from far below, came solemn warning from currents finding their way in the darkness.

A place of mystic enchantment. How he hated to leave, though the leaning walls threatened him and he shivered in the cold! Once more at the top, he noted huge stones, riding the glacier on their age-long journey, a journey of more than a hundred years, without a single stop, winter or summer.

The next day John returned to the Valley, excited, but sobered, by the task ahead. Other glaciers—there must be many more—protected by the cool shadows of the cliffs, still carving the sculpture of the Sierra, as their giant forerunners had done. He would find them, measure them, time their motion and advance. Patiently, painfully, even dangerously, he would assemble his facts. Let Whitney rant and the fawning geologists follow him; he, John Muir, would know the secrets of the mountains.

Winter again. Muir was caretaker at Black's Hotel. With the tourists gone, the Valley filled with snow, the wind howling outside his door, he sat warm and snug inside his new cabin. This was the time he needed, he told himself. Before him lay untouched sheets of paper. Beside him ink and a well-sharpened quill. But all around his feet were scattered balls of paper, once promising, now discarded. No, this writing business was not so simple!

On the fifth of December his article had come out in the *New York Herald Tribune*. "The Death of a Glacier," he had called it, but in the paper it was "Yosemite Glaciers." He was proud of his clipping and kept it where his eye could light on it. Perhaps he might earn his living by the pen?

It was hard to choose a subject, harder still to find the words, which was queer. For words were no strangers to him. He was a fluent talker. And words flowed easily into his notebooks, vivid words that gave the mood of the moment or every detail of a mountain picture. Where had they gone—those words? The ones that came to him now seemed dull, "hard and bony." He was caught by self-consciousness. What to say? How to say it?

He picked up his quill and chewed viciously on the upper end. If he chewed one end, the words sometimes came out the other, he thought. All his life he had made his own pens, chiefly from goose feathers. His mother's gray goose had yielded many. But this pen was different. He took out his pocketknife and sharpened the nib again, bringing it to a finer point.

He remembered well where he had found this quill. Standing one day on the shoulder of Mt. Hoffman, he had felt a shadow pass over him and, looking up, saw a great eagle swooping in majestic curves. He knew it was a golden eagle by the black underpart and the gleam of white at the end of its tail. Fascinated, he watched the master of wind and space, uplifted by the sight of so much strength and beauty. Then, as he started to hike on, he saw a single feather lying in the snow at his feet.

The quill from a golden eagle! Surely, he thought, this should bring power to his writing, but today the magic failed. Through the following days John struggled at his task, telling himself grimly, *I will learn to write.*

In December nature herself came to his rescue and provided a subject. A great, three-day storm swept the Yosemite, flooding the Valley. His vivid description of it the *Tribune* accepted as "Yosemite in Winter." Then came the spring night when John was awakened by the rattling of his cabin windows, a tremor in the air, a deep, ominous rumble. Frightened, he ran out the door to find the moonlit meadow in convulsions under his feet, with shocks so wild there seemed no stable place in which to stand, no safety in the land.

Fear—yes—yet a curious exaltation seized him, a sense of joy that he could witness this upheaval of nature. Carried away with excitement, he leapt upon a great boulder, waving his arms and shouting, "A noble earthquake!" Now the shocks became more and more violent till he feared that Sentinel Rock, towering above his cabin, would fall to crush it, that the Great Wall itself might collapse, bringing them all to a common doom. Then he saw it falling—Eagle Rock on the south wall, plunging forward in a shower of boulders with a tremendous roar, sweeping to the floor of the Valley in a long, luminous arc of flame.

When John whipped his account of the earthquake into shape, he sent it to the *Tribune*, which accepted it at once. On May 7th it appeared as "Yosemite in Spring." By the beginning of summer, he had really embarked on writing. He began a series for the *Overland Monthly*, easily the outstanding journal of the Pacific Coast, which had published Ambrose Bierce and Mark Twain. Bret Harte was its first editor.

Success in writing, joy in his explorations—this was a heady brew which gave a lift to the spirit!

Spring became summer. Just as John began to feel that

the eagle's quill was under control, quiet in which to write was gone. Now came John Tyndall, famous English geologist, then Asa Gray, leading botanist of Harvard. But it was for the coming of Agassiz, master of them all, that John had long been hoping. Mrs. Carr sent word the great teacher was on his way to San Francisco and wished above all to study the Sierra.

In August word came that Agassiz was in the city, too tired and sick to visit the mountains. Deeply disappointed, John sent him a "long, icy letter," telling him of the "glorious things he had to show him." The answer was in Mrs. Agassiz's handwriting. She wrote that her husband had said, "Here is the first man I have ever found who has any adequate idea of glacial action." She added, "He says he will visit you next summer."

But the younger man never met the great master, to whom he owed so much of his knowledge, and Agassiz never learned how much John was in debt to him. By next summer Louis Agassiz was dead.

October and Indian summer. John had just come down from the headwaters of the Tuolumne, a region of towering peaks and smooth, alpine meadows, aflame with autumn beauty. As he gazed at them, he had longed to be an artist with colors and brush. Now it was good to find the peace of his cabin again.

As he neared it, little Floy Hutchings, whom he called "Squirrel," came capering along the trail with two men behind her.

"Friends looking for you," she cried and was off with

a bound, before he could thank her. For a moment John was annoyed. He was weary, footsore, and hungry. Was this another meaningless interruption?

"Mr. Muir?" The elder of the two men held out his hand with the usual letter from Mrs. Carr. "My name's Keith. I bring you a note of introduction from . . ."

"Oh, yes, I know!" John answered with a smile, which turned into a laugh as he read the message. "I commission this artist to sketch you in your hayrope suspenders, against the day when you are famous."

Muir took note of the man before him, of the sturdy frame, fine, intelligent face, and brilliant eyes; also of his stock in trade—canvas, paintbox, and brushes.

"By your name, a Scotsman?"

"Aye."

"And a Hielander?"

"Aye, brither, a Hielander!"

From that moment John and William Keith were friends.

The artists told John they wished to go to the summit range, to find something unusual, individual, and picturesque. John thought of the beautiful place which had given him such joy the day before, and promised to take them there.

"Give me a blink of rest, time in which to choose a good pack mule. I'll show you the crown of the Sierra," he cried, remembering his own longing to be an artist.

At last, toward the end of their second day of climbing, they rounded a projecting headland and the whole picture stood revealed in the flush of the alpenglow—a cluster of snowclad peaks surging free into the sky from the head of a magnificent valley.

For a moment Keith stood gazing, transfixed in silence. Then, all Scotch reserve forgotten, he dashed forward, shouting and waving his arms. As John went to work cutting pine boughs for beds, the artists rushed about like irresponsible children, choosing spots from which to paint.

High against the darkness the campfire roared up and they made their plans for the time ahead. Food would last for several days. Working from many angles would keep them occupied. John said he would like to take a trip to the untouched summit of Mt. Ritter and they at once urged him to go. Only a day's journey to the foot of the mountain, he told them. The weather calm; not much chance of snow.

"But will you return in time?" Irwin asked him anxiously. "Are you sure? What if you were ill or hurt or trapped by a storm?"

"I am never ill or hurt," John answered proudly. "As for storm, the real danger is snow. But I could weather one and so could you. Keep up big fires and wait till I come. One thing you must promise me," he added. "If I should be late, if a blizzard should overwhelm you, do not try to reach the Valley alone!"

"We do so promise!" Keith answered gravely, raising a right hand as if he were in a court of law.

The next morning before dawn John started out, with fire in his veins and joy in his heart. Mastering Mt. Ritter would be no child's play, for it was king of the central portion of the High Sierra, as Shasta was of the North and Whitney of the South; 13,300 feet of tortuous, difficult climbing. So far as he knew, the summit had never been reached. Clarence King, Whitney's assistant, had tried it and failed. That made it all the more tempting!

All his first day was pure pleasure. About a mile from camp he came to a white cascade, beating its way down a rugged gorge in a canyon side. Gladly he climbed along it, liking its wild music, the taste of spray in his face. "Higher, higher. New beauty everywhere. Painted meadows, strange peaks, lakes shining like silver, and far, far down beyond the range, the Mono Desert lying silent in thick, purple light."

When evening came and "long, blue, spiky shadows crept out across the snow fields," while the peaks turned rose color in the alpenglow, he was still miles away from Mt. Ritter. He found a good camp ground on the rim of a glacier basin. A lake, deep in the center of it, furnished water for tea, while low, scraggly pines, anchored in the rocks, gave him shelter for his bed. Creeping into the pine thicket, he found dun-colored sparrows nesting there. The night wind grew bitter cold, rose to a rough gale. Almost freezing without blankets, he slipped out often to his fire. Breakfast was bread and tea. A hard crust, tied to his belt, his only food for the climb. The rest he secured carefully against marauding wood rats.

Ritter was fully in sight as he pushed rapidly on, his ironshod shoes making a clanking sound. Descending to a glacier at his left, he crossed it diagonally upward. Then, picking his holds with intense caution, scanning its face again and again, he began to scale the sheer, ice-covered precipice that towered at the head of the glacier.

Halfway to the top now, inching his way slowly upward. Handholds and footholds became fewer. Projecting roughness vanished. Suddenly he was brought to a dead stop with arms outspread, clinging to the face of the smooth, perpendicular cliff. Impossible to climb further, impossible to retreat. His doom seemed certain: he must fall. For the first time in his mountain life, hope was gone. Bewildered, shaking in terror, his mind seemed to fill with a stifling smoke. Only one thing was certain—death lay below. Then the eclipse passed. A new sense seemed to possess him. The other self—experience, instinct, guardian angel—came forward and took control of him. Now strong arms held him; wings seemed to lift him up. Every rift and flaw in the rock was seen as through a microscope, and he climbed with a sureness and precision for which he was not responsible. Though the way to the top now led through a maze of yawning chasms and gullies, the strange influx of strength continued, till at last he stood on the highest crag in the brilliant sunlight. In his first hour of freedom from the terrible shadow behind him, the warm and friendly sunshine seemed reward enough.

Safely back in the Valley with the two artists in tow, Muir often thought of his experience on Mt. Ritter. Was it inner strength that helped him in the crisis, or had some power beyond himself intervened to save him? Groping to express his wonder, he wrote in his Journal:

"The life of a mountaineer seems to be particularly favorable to soul-life, as well as limb-life. . . . We little suspect the capacity that even our flesh has for knowledge. . . . My legs sometimes transport me to camp in the darkness, over cliffs and through bogs and forests that seem inaccessible to civilized legs in the daylight."

Had the "knowledge of the flesh" then saved him?

But Muir, mystic and believer in the God of nature, also wrote in his notes, "If a magnetic needle, a strip or particle of iron be shown its way, shall the soul of a free man be left unguided?"

The month before John climbed Mt. Ritter, LeConte, the scientist, gave a paper before the California Academy of Sciences. Its title was "Some Ancient Glaciers of the Sierra," and it was the first published account of Muir's discoveries. In the two years since John found his first glacier, he had added sixty-five others to his list. These, despite the world's scepticism and Whitney's scorn, he had found, measured, observed, and proved to be still in flow.

Now LeConte took it upon himself to present these findings to the scientific world. True, he gave full credit to Muir for the original idea and for further work, but the paper was so full of LeConte and his own explorations that the credit to Muir was like the well-known needle, lost in the hay. Mrs. Carr was disturbed and urged John to publish his own report—at once. "Other men, less scrupulous than LeConte, will establish claim to all your own original, creative work. Do stop your eternal letter writing and publish *now!*"

Dr. Carr agreed with her, and John knew that they were right, but he lingered in the Sierra until the following fall, when he made a final, unhappy decision. Yes, he would go down to the city and give his full time to writing, for how could he work on a book with all the life of the mountains to call him? Now came a ten months' stay in the Bay cities—time which he afterwards called, "that strange Oakland epoch."

The day was cold, snowflakes were whirling over the granite walls when John shouldered his few possessions and started away. Mr. and Mrs. J. B. McChesney, who lived in Oakland, made him welcome. A single room in another man's home! Well, he had had that experience before; but the change from Yosemite was overwhelming. He hated the noise and confusion of cities, the pale and listless people of the streets, from whose faces happiness never shone, the heavy air of the low country. Each morning, fog rolled in from the sea to choke and stifle him. But he was lost in an even heavier fog.

I will learn to write, he had boasted earlier. Yet still the right words would not come. They "rattled like dry bones." They were but "mist-rags" of poor expression. He had contracted for a series of sketches for the *Over-*

land Monthly. "Studies in the Sierra," he named it, and it was to tell the entire story of his mountain explorations. It must be done!

Only one thing redeemed this time of exile for Muir— the kindness of friends. The Carrs lived nearby and they tried to help him. William Keith, the artist, came over from San Francisco, or John went to see him. And he added a new friend, one who was to mean more than most to his future life, John Swett, the plucky State Superintendent, who had fought the bosses and made California schools outstanding in the States.

Swett and Keith both listened to John's work, offering much friendly criticism.

"Too rigid," said Swett, as he frowned over a badly written sentence.

"I know it!" poor John cried in despair. "But how shall I say it?"

"Wait!" Keith interrupted. "Tell us that whole episode, just as if we were hearing it for the first time—talk it to us. You're a grand talker!"

"That's good," Swett agreed. "Now go home and write it down."

Later, in Dr. Carr's house, Muir met three new friends —the Strenzels, father, mother, and daughter. Dr. Strenzel, physician and horticulturist, had come as an exile from Europe many years before and now lived on his beautiful fruit-growing acres in the hill country back of Oakland. John was delighted with the older man who asked so many keen and eager questions, but all through the evening his eyes kept straying to the lovely face of the girl who sat quietly beside him. She listened—and missed nothing, John could see that. Once their glances met and as he gazed deeply into the wide-set gray eyes, with their look of candor and understanding, suddenly he knew how lonely he was. "Louie Wanda." Later that night he turned the queer foreign name over and over on his lips, liking the music it made.

Winter lengthened into spring, summer was nearing fall. John felt weary, half sick, desperately in need of mountain air and freedom, but—the manuscript on the table was growing fast. Finally, in September, he took the last of his "Sierra Studies" into Avery's office. But where was the relief and triumph? Where the happiness he needed?

Walking down one of the less busy streets, he wandered half dazed, hardly seeing the faces of people as he passed. They were all more or less sick, he thought. Was there ever a sane man in the big city? He himself was like the boy who had been caught in a deep well years ago, almost losing his life in the fatal chokedamp. Could he escape now, or had city fumes caught him with their deadly poison?

Then in an empty lot full of weeds, he saw a stretch of pure mountain beauty. Goldenrod, the tasseled heads lifted in the sun, as lovely as the ones that grew in Sierra meadows! Now he knew how sick he was, how desperate. Only one place could heal him. That night he packed in feverish haste—and fled to the mountains.

9

The Incomparable Valley

BACK AT LAST IN THE YOSEMITE, JOHN FELT THAT LIFE was good again. Relief and joy seemed to flow in to him from every wind that blew; from Tissiack, "towering like a God," from the beautiful, sunlit valley. But gradually his mood changed. Had he not finished his work here? And tied all the results of his explorations into a neat bundle of words?

Baffled by his own inconsistencies, John wrote again to Mrs. Carr. He told her of the long trip "home," of the strange climax, the curious sense of emptiness, which replaced his joy.

No one of the rocks seems to call me now, nor any of the distant mountains . . . I will not try to tell the Valley yet. I feel that I am a stranger here. I shall go out in a day or so. Farewell! Keep this goldenrod and yarrow. They are old lang syne.

Ever lovingly yours,
John Muir.

* * *

Had John turned against the place which he really loved best of all? It was not so easy to leave, he found, as he made the rounds of all his favorite haunts—Glacier Rock, the Great Fall, the Mariposa Grove. But the mood lingered. He felt that his work was done, a chapter of his life closed. He had proved his glacial theory, written his findings and sent them in for publication. Now a wider world must claim him, other interests, other causes. What Mrs. Carr called "John Muir's daemon" was once more in the saddle. Yet, to the end of his life, he was to be the great defender of "the Incomparable Valley."

By late October John was off on another excursion, going by Lake Tahoe toward the Northwest. Here he was saddened and angered at the sight of pines and firs crashing down every skid row. At nearby Lake Donner he found the whole edge of the forest hacked and thinned. Something like a cold rage seemed to grow and grow in his heart, hardening into a fixed resolve. Someone must make the people of California understand the value of their forests. Value not in cold dollars and cents, but as a heritage of beauty, health, and joy, irreplaceable when lost. As a reservoir of their water supply also, much needed in this arid land.

Lover of trees that he was, he would have saved each one for its own sake, but he was also a scientist. He knew that the destruction of forests would mean floods in the rivers, the depletion of soil, would lead to the whole unbalance of the land. Was destiny giving him another cause? Soon, he told himself—when he could—he must make a careful study of the Sierra groves.

On to the North now, following the main Oregon and California stage road from Redding to Sisson's Station. No aimless wander this, for Shasta, king of the northern range, was his main objective. He had climbed Mt. Ritter. How could he leave Shasta unconquered? When he first saw it in the distance he was still fifty miles away, alone, afoot, exhausted. But all his blood "turned to wine and weariness left him."

At Sisson's he tried to persuade some mountaineer to share the climb, but one by one they refused. "Too late in the season. Snow ten feet deep. You'll be caught by a blizzard, buried, and freeze to death." Undaunted, John persuaded a local man, Jerome Fay, to take blankets and a week's supply of rations up on horseback, as far as they could break through the snow. At the timber line he made camp and Fay returned. On November second he reached the "utmost summit," spent two hours tracing lava channels and the pathways of glaciers, then returned to camp before dark. A bitter wind rose; every sign showed a storm was brewing. Digging himself in deeply in the lee of a great lava block, with a pile of wood beside him, a warm fire, and blankets, he waited for the blizzard to come. The world next day was a whirling tempest of white, but John, snug and secure, studied this Shasta storm with joy. Yes, he could stretch his food supply to last two or even three weeks!

The ways of small animals—a squirrel, mountain sheep;

the coming of a "fine Clark crow"; the depth of snow, velocity of the wind, all these details he recorded in his notebook. "Three inches of snow on my blankets." "Glorious storm!" To his vast disgust, a rescue party, sent by Sisson, came to take him down on the fifth day.

In the following weeks Muir managed to circle the whole base of the mountain and sent an account of it to the *San Francisco Evening Bulletin*. Then on to Brownsville, where Emily Pelton was staying. Would the old attachment ripen into love? Perhaps in this winter visit he might find an answer.

The Knox home, where Emily was living, stood on a divide between the Yuba and Feather Rivers. Cordially she greeted him and made him welcome. But from the first, he had a sense that there was something lacking. Not the warmth he had longed for.

Had he offended her? Proved wanting in some way? Did she think him queer, or unreliable? People sometimes did, he reflected sadly. But still he stayed on, wistfully trying to find the old relationship.

This was a strange December, warm but stormy. There came a day when a great wind suddenly attacked the forests and shook the house with battering blows.

"A wonderful storm!" John cried, rushing for the front door. But Emily was there before him. Clinging to him with both hands, she begged him not to be so wild and foolish, exposing himself to danger, making them all anxious.

"Nonsense!" John answered, twisting himself away.

"At least, take this," she said, whipping an old coat off its hook, one which belonged to their host. "Put it on!"

John took it with a mixture of amusement and disdain, and dashed out the door.

Not for the world would he have missed this experience, for here was a chance to study a great forest under terrible stress. Yet far more than that! From some mysterious depths within him, which he hardly understood, rose an urgency, an emotional need to meet and exult in the passion of the storm.

Fighting his way through the woods, body bent against the wind, he heard the crashing of trees as they fell beside him. Still he rushed on, sometimes stopping in the lee of a rock to catch his breath, to watch and hear the wild tumult about him. Even above the organ tones of the wind, he caught, or thought he caught, the tones of different trees—spruce and fir and pine and leafless oak, or the long rustle of the grasses at his feet.

Toward midday, having reached the highest ridge, he found a Douglas spruce to climb, one hundred feet tall, with branches not too far from the ground, choosing it carefully for its youth and strength. A tree climber from childhood, he slowly mastered it, getting traction from the spikes in his shoes, depending on the iron strength of his arms. The top of it bent and swirled, backward and forward, while he clung with muscles braced, "like a bobolink on a reed."

In its widest sweep his tree top described an arc of from twenty to thirty degrees, but he felt sure of its

elastic strength. Had he not seen spruces bent to the ground by snow, still unbroken? Safe, he rode the waving top, "taking the wind into his pulses," watching the excited forest.

He kept his lofty perch for hours, often closing his eyes to listen to the storm music, or to feast on fragrance carried by the wind; scents brought from afar, bearing the salt of distant seas, the breath of flowery meadows, the pungent odor of sequoia and pine. Winds are the great travelers, he thought, telling their wanderings by their scents alone.

But not until this moment, swinging in the wind, had he ever realized that "trees were travelers too." They could make journeys, though not extensive ones. "Yet the little journeys of men, away and back again, were they so much more important than tree wavings after all?"

"A Wind-Storm in the Forest of the Yuba" became one of John's best known, best loved sketches. When, much later, it appeared in *Scribner's Monthly* many people wrote to him. Anthologies and readers included it until it became a chapter in his first book, "The Mountains of California."

It was not strange that as he left Emily it was with the understanding that they would "always be friends." But nothing more, John realized, with a mixture of pain and relief. She thought him wild and unpredictable. She would never understand him. And how could he tie himself to a tame and settled pussycat?

Back in San Francisco, Muir settled down in the big, three-storied home of John Swett. His was a charming family, complete with both grandmothers, two children, and a new baby about to arrive. When she appeared, John helped to name her Helen. In these days he tried to work at his writing. Again he turned for advice to his wise schoolmaster friend. What next and how?

"Why not aim at one of the eastern magazines?" asked Swett, sliding a brown pipe out of his mouth and squinting at him shrewdly. "It's all very well to publish out here in the West, but we haven't the influence. If *Scribner's* or *Harper's* had taken your glacial stuff, your theories would have been accepted long ago!"

Following his advice, John reworked and sent to *Harper's* his article on "Living Glaciers." It was published in November of that year.

In these spring days, as he sat at his desk, his thoughts slid away to the mountains. The eagle's quill lay quiet; new ideas were left dangling; blue eyes, looking out at a city which they failed to see, had indeed a faraway look. Once more he stood in the quiet of a sequoia grove, seeing the great trees with their lofty, plumed tops and beautiful reddish trunks, serene and ageless. They had grown in peace and beauty long before Christ was born. Then he saw hacked and splintered logs sliding down the skid rows and heard the roar of exploding dynamite. First and foremost and always on his mind now was the need to know what was happening to the forests. Yes, he thought, as soon as he could manage it, he would visit all the sequoia groves and see for himself.

By the end of July John was guiding two men, Washburn and Bagley of San Francisco, down the range toward Mt. Whitney. Camping in the Kings River Yosemite on the South Fork, they found it as beautiful, though not as striking as the Merced Yosemite, "the Incomparable Valley." But it was wild and untouched in its loveliness and Muir was filled with resentment when he found a notice nailed to one of the pines.

> We, the undersigned, claim this valley for the purpose of raising stock.
>
> Thomas, Richard, Harvey and Co.

There was no question in Muir's mind what to write when he sent in his letter of protest and appeal to the *San Francisco Bulletin*. "The Merced Yosemite has all its wild gardens now trampled by cows and horses. . . . All the destructible beauty of this remote Kings River Yosemite is doomed to perish like that of its neighbor."

At the same time he sent a letter to Mrs. Carr, saying, "I want to go with the sequoias a month or two, into all their homes from North to South." By mid-August he was carrying out his plan. Alone with a small brown mule, named for its own color, John followed the range for two and a half months through the finest part of the Sierra forests. For one hundred and eighty miles the sequoia groves stretched in a broken belt along the west flank of the mountains.

Brownie was a wonderful companion, tough, gentle and, for a mule, obedient. John thought he appreciated his vocal efforts, with a preference for the Scotch. When "It's up wi' the Bonnets o' Bonnie Dundee" rent the air, he pricked up his floppy ears and seemed to jog along in time.

This was no idle wander, for John filled his note-books with careful estimates—extent and condition of groves, height, width, and probable age of trees, amount of destruction. And side by side with scientific facts stood some of the most lyric of all his tributes to nature.

"A supremely noble tree, the redwood was once more widely distributed, but not the *Sequoia Gigantea*. They are the most venerable looking of all the Sierra giants, standing erect and true, in poise so perfect they seem to make no effort, their strength so perfect it is invisible. Brown and gray and yellow-lichened . . . they stand sound and serene after the hardships of wind and weather of five thousand years. Towering to the dimness of a cathedral spire, no other tree has seen so much, none is so full of other days. Scores of centuries of sunshine are in it. Some are still standing older than the pyramids."

On the divide south of Kings River, John came upon Hyde's sawmill, "booming and moaning like a bad ghost, destroying many a fine tree . . . two million feet of lumber this year and it has been running three years. When felled, the sequoia breaks like glass, from twenty-five to fifty percent unfit for the mill." Evil waste, he saw, was added to destruction.

Further southward now, to the Tule Basin, where John found another magnificent sequoia grove. But progress was hampered by Brownie, who grew listless and slow. Sometimes he was caught in chaparral and had to be helped out; sometimes he set his four feet down and refused to budge.

One night as Muir sat by his campfire, ready for his supper of tea with an unleavened cake, he felt a nose push his shoulder and heard a pathetic bray. Then he understood! The poor beast was starving. Every night he had been turned out to forage, but the meadows had been swept clean by sheep. That night Brownie had the supper and Muir the tea. The next day they went down to the lowlands to buy and bring back a sack of barley.

Everywhere John went he talked to the men of the mountains—farmers, millers, or sheepmen—for he was anxious to see the overall picture. He learned that water sources had been grabbed by speculators and mill owners, that farmers had to pay for water. Fighting poverty and drought, their only hope lay in organizing to secure their rights. Muir knew that the saving of the watershed forests was essential, if there was to be any farming left in the valleys.

Back in San Francisco that winter, the eagle's quill needed no urging. John wrote an article for the *Record-Union* of Sacramento. The title was a question—"How Shall We Preserve our Forests?" Moved by his own anger and sense of need, he tried to appeal to "practical men."

He protested against the ruthless waste of sawmills, with their strip lumbering, the desolation left by flocks of greedy "hoofed locusts" (as he called sheep), against the running fires set by sheepmen. Of all the scourges perhaps fire was the worst, for it destroyed young trees, especially the loose-barked sequoias. *"Soon there will be no forests left."*

John knew well the menace of fire, for he had just stood in a sequoia grove where "flames came rushing like devouring lions . . . every living thing flaming." John hoped his vivid article might reach the legislators. At the end of it he wrote, "Whether our loose-limbed government is willing to do anything in this matter remains to be seen." He closed with the suggestion that a careful survey of the forests be made. Probably no legislators read his words, but nature lovers and conservationists began to rally to Muir's cause and hail him as a leader.

It was not till twenty-one years later that his idea of a forest survey bore fruit. Then President Cleveland set up a commission to study the forest areas of the United States. Men like Sargent and Pinchot were on it, and Muir, traveling from coast to coast, was its chief adviser.

As John's articles began to be more widely read, invitations to lecture added to his influence. The old debater of college days came to the fore. He spoke with force when he defended his glacial theory or protested the ruin of the wilderness.

It was two years later. John stood on a bank of the

Sacramento, where the sloping land of Rancho Chico touched the stream. Wistfully his eyes followed the sweeping reaches of the river; then he turned to General Bidwell who stood beside him.

"Wish I could sail down it."

"Well, why not? Tell you what, Muir, I'll have my carpenter build you a boat. But I'm sorry," he added, "you wish to leave so soon."

"How could I ever wish to leave Rancho Chico? You and Mrs. Bidwell have been kindness itself!"

First it was the *Chico Flagship*, then christened the *Spoonbill*, but at any rate a peculiar craft, half canoe, half skiff. John sailed merrily off in it, flags flying at bow and stern, a week's load of rations stashed away, and one of Mrs. Bidwell's old quilts to keep off the night chill.

Snags and hidden logs were common, but the little boat slid over them so cleverly that John re-named her *Snag-jumper*, soon shortened to *Snag*. Once she sprang a bad leak, but he rowed her to shore in time. Whittling the boards smooth with his jackknife, he pounded them tight with a heavy stone. Now she was seaworthy and in due time they reached Sacramento. Here John left his skiff with a wharf man who had boats of his own. In return he was guided into town through the darkness by way of the "Barbary Coast." "Lucky ye be," the old fellow said to him in parting, "I ain't a-murthered you here in the dark!"

Weary of his cramped legs, John, by sure instinct, went up to the Sierra. Here he followed a difficult route through the Middle Fork Valley of the Kings River, long called inaccessible. It was merely rough going for John's mountain legs. Soon he reached the Merced River at Hopeton and decided to take to the water again. This time he made his own boat, with some twisted fence rails, a bag of ancient nails, and another big stone. As he launched *Snag the Second*, then rowed from the Merced into the San Joaquin, he had no advance knowledge or premonition that this was to prove the most momentous voyage of his life.

10

Alaska and
the Lost Glacier

JOHN MUIR'S SAIL DOWN TWO RIVERS, TO THE SPOT WHERE
the Sacramento and San Joaquin joined, left him hungry
and weary. He rejoiced when he reached the docks off
Martinez—and wondered why. Then he remembered.
Mrs. Carr's "Strenzel trinity" lived here, didn't they, the
pleasant people who had urged him to call? A place called
Alhambra Valley? He strode off on his long legs without
a backward glance at abandoned *Snag*.

Dr. John Strenzel, physician and fruit grower, once in-
volved in a Polish rebellion against Russia, looked out of
the window of his house one November day at a bedrag-
gled-looking man walking up his driveway. Even from a
distance he could see the wrinkled suit, with a sleeve so
torn that a bare elbow protruded, and thought that a
tramp must be coming to beg. Then he noted the swift
stride, the vigor and assurance, the copper-colored hair,
and knew his visitor at once.

Throwing the door wide, he welcomed John with
warmth. "Mr. Muir, this is indeed an honor! Come in!

Come in! I've just been reading your last article in the *Bulletin*. Mother, Louie, come! Here's Mr. Muir!"

Mrs. Strenzel swept forward to lay a motherly hand on the unkempt sleeve, and John for the first time was aware of his own appearance. "Afraid I'm pretty disreputable— but . . ."

"You've been off on an adventure? We want to hear about it."

Then Louie, small and charming, slipped out of the shadows and smiled up at him, the warm flush deepening a little on her cheeks. "Mr. Muir, it's been a long time, hasn't it,—three years since we met you? I'm glad you've come."

John stared at her in amazement. How different she was from the quiet, listening girl he had seen at Mrs. Carr's! A woman of maturity and poise, and beauty. He smiled down at her.

"I wonder why it's been so long," he said.

All the Strenzels bestirred themselves to make John feel at home. Mrs. Strenzel came with a plate of sliced turkey, while Louie brought a tray of chiming glasses filled with vintage port. The good doctor rushed for his best blend of tobacco.

"This was my first rest in six weeks. They pitied my weary looks and made me eat and sleep, stuffing me with chicken, turkey, beef, fruits, and jellies in the most extravagant manner. And they begged me to stay a month," John wrote to Sarah.

It was hard, he found, to tear himself away. As he stood

in the doorway, saying good-by, he clung to Louie's hand a trifle overlong.

"I'll be back soon," he promised, and meant it this time from the bottom of his heart.

Walking back to Oakland across the top of Mt. Diablo, he was soon at the Swetts' house in San Francisco.

"Where have you been this time?" asked Mary, with the stay-at-home's envy of the traveler.

"Oh, down two rivers to Martinez."

"Martinez? Did you happen to see the Strenzels?"

"Why, yes, I did. Stayed there for two days, in fact."

"Enjoyed it?"

"Immensely. The doctor is a real scientist. We talked for half the night."

"And did you happen to see a young lady there?"

"Um—well—yes, there was a young lady about the house."

Helen Swett, noting John's torn and faded coat, his rumpled hair, sadly in need of cutting, wished that the beautiful Louie had not seen him in such a plight. She need not have worried. For the wise, observant Louie had noticed other things.

That winter in San Francisco John had more fun with his writing. The criticism of the Swetts helped; even more the gay youngsters, John and Frank and Helen, who made "Uncle John" tell them stories. Simple drama in good vivid form came easily to him now, and he used the same art in his sketches.

When the "Humming Bird of the California Waterfalls" went in to *Scribner's*, the editors asked him to send them all his future work. Other sketches followed fast. Robert Underwood Johnson, later the editor of *Century Magazine*, charmed by them and impressed by the man who wrote them, became a devoted friend.

Perhaps more than all the rest, the small flame flickering in John's heart, the new hope of happiness ahead, added to his creative power. And often through the winter and early spring of 1878 he dropped his quill to stride across the Oakland hills to the welcome he was so sure of finding.

In June he was captured by wanderlust again. When Captain A. F. Rodgers asked him to join the Coast and Geodetic Survey going to Nevada and the Great Basin, he accepted at once. Taking time to say good-by to the Strenzels, he found the elders opposed to his going. "The Indians are so dangerous," Mrs. Strenzel protested. But John, who feared neither man nor rattlesnake, only smiled. Louie, he noticed, kept quiet while her parents talked, and he felt a sudden fresh respect for her. Could this possibly be a woman who would leave a man free?

From Nevada John took time to write long, chatty letters.

Dear Strenzels:

All goes well in camp. All the Indians we meet are as harmless as sagebushes, though perhaps as bitter at heart. . . . The wild brier roses are in full bloom, sweeter and bonnier far than Louie's best, bonnie though they be. . . . I can see no post office nearer than Austin, Nevada, three weeks away. The packs are afloat.

> Good morning. J. M.

One significant thing came out of this trip to Nevada. Making a careful study of glacial action near Mt. Jefferson in the Toquima Mountains, he sent his findings to the *San Francisco Bulletin*, which published them on December 5. This article contained frequent allusions to "more than one glacial winter."

Even to the end of Muir's life and beyond, critics were apt to say of his glacial theory about the Yosemite, "For a man of his time he came pretty close to the truth, but of course he failed to realize that there was more than one glacial period." But Muir did know it and went on record as knowing it in the winter of 1878.

Through the years, John Muir's conception of the glacial origin of the Yosemite met with scepticism, even contempt. Still the scientists held that the deep U-shape of the Valley was produced by cataclysm or water erosion, not by ice action. But gradually they began to sing a different tune. It remained for François E. Mathes of the United States Geological Survey, eminent authority on glacial action in the Sierra, to write in 1930:

"The ice age, it is now clear, was preceded in the Sierra by long periods of canyon cutting by water, but let no one cite this fact to Muir's discredit, for no man of his time, however expert, could have proved this. . . . It is now certain, upon reading Muir's letters and other writings, that he was more intimately familiar with the facts on the ground, and more nearly right in their interpretation, than any geologist of his time."

Elsewhere Mathes writes, "It was John Muir who first saw clearly that the glaciers themselves had done most of the excavating."

More recently, depth findings (by 85 seismic reflection tests) were made on the floor of Yosemite Valley by two distinguished geologists: Buwalda of the California Institute of Technology and Blackwelder of Stanford University. They proved that the bottom of Lake Yosemite, once in the floor of the Valley, was 1800 to 2000 feet below the present floor, though previously thought to be 200 feet.

"These findings have added the most powerful and convincing evidence to support Muir's assertions that glaciers were the major eroding agents in the formation of Yosemite and other great Sierra canyons," writes William E. Colby in *Yosemite Nature Notes* of January 1956. Only ice could have carved so deeply.

It is now recognized that John Muir told the truth in saying: "When we walk the pathways of Yosemite glaciers and observe their separate works—the mountains they have shaped, the canyons they have furrowed, the rocks they have worn—on reaching Yosemite itself, instead of being overwhelmed by its greatness we ask, 'Is this all?' wondering that so mighty a concentration of energy did not find yet grander expression."

Time—and further knowledge—have vindicated John Muir.

The earth turned. It was April again and John was back in San Francisco. He began to write his first personal letters to Louie.

Dear Miss Strenzel: (They were still amazingly formal.)
The other day I chanced to find in my pocket that slippery, fuzzy mesh you wear over your head. . . .

Why had the fascinator slipped from Louie's head as they took an evening walk together? Why had John come away with it in his pocket? This, certainly, was a sign of spring!

But John still had work to do. Paid one hundred dollars in advance, he went to give two talks on "Glacial Action in the Yosemite" before a big convention meeting in the Valley. Other famous speakers were there, but the *San Francisco Chronicle* gave its "rave notice" to John Muir. "This speaker fairly electrified his audience and over a hundred followed him up the Eagle Point Trail. . . . This was fun for him, for he leaped over the crags like a goat."

At the same convention Dr. Sheldon Jackson, head of the Indian Missions in Alaska, spoke glowingly of the North Country. John listened entranced. He had already

made plans for a new trip, to see the Puget Sound region, the Olympics, and the "Mountain-which-is-God,"
as the Indians called Mt. Rainier. Now he added Alaska
to his list, filled with an eagerness to leave at once.

It was the day before his departure when he went to
say good-by at Martinez. Dr. Strenzel met him at the
door, waving a newspaper. "Hail, the Conquering Hero
comes!" he cried, much to John's confusion. That evening he drew Louie out of the house into the warmth
of the night, past the live oaks, the vineyards, the rows
and rows of pear and cherry trees, marching like regiments
across the land. Moonlight flooded the beautiful valley
and gave a mystic charm to Louie's roses. As she stooped
over them, touching them softly, John thought that he
had never seen anything lovelier than the light in her face.

Hand in hand they walked on, silent, happy, completely content—on to the open country, where high,
rolling hills lay silver-white, with deep pools of darkness
between.

"Darling . . ." John turned and took Louie in his arms.

Later, much later, when they began to talk, he told
her slowly of his heartbreak at leaving her. "I can hardly
bear . . ." but Louie reached up a hand and stopped the
words.

"Don't—not tonight. And never think that I shall fail
to understand. It's your work—exploring. I know that!
Love shouldn't be a cage. I'll try . . ."

But he silenced her with his lips. She was fire in his
blood; she was the deepest hunger he had ever known.

That night Louie slipped into Mrs. Strenzel's room and laid her cool cheek down on her mother's. The old lady stirred, asked sleepily, "What's wrong, dear?"

"Wrong? Oh, no! Everything is completely right now, Mother."

The next day John stood on the deck of the *Dakota*, as she steamed slowly through the Golden Gate and headed for open sea. Beside him his traveling companion, Thomas Magee of San Francisco, gestured and pointed, while crowds milled around them. But soon the deck was deserted and even his friend, with a sheepish backward glance, hurried below.

John stood alone, watching the long, gray, breaking waves, liking the quivering rise of the steamer's bow, its sudden plunge; liking the salt spray on his lips, the wind in his face. Gulls and albatrosses, "strong, glad life in the midst of stormy beauty," skimmed the waves, while far to the left six great whales moved slowly by, their backs like granite boulders rising from the sea. Now they spouted lustily and disappeared.

Exulting, thrilled, John felt the years slip away. Again he was a lad rushing into the whitecaps on the Dunbar coast. He was the older boy who stood at the bow of another steamer, heading for a land he had never seen. New lands, new conquest! Swift and sure, all his love of adventure returned.

From Victoria, the small, old-fashioned, very English capital of British Columbia, John saw the whole magnificent range of the Olympics outlined southward. From

Tacoma, far up, incredibly far up in the sky, he caught the gleaming cone of Mt. Rainier, separated from earth by swirling mists, only the peak visible. The Mountain-which-is-God, no wonder the Indians named it so!

With a rush of envy, he wished that he had been the first to master it. Only once climbed as yet—he knew that! Another time, he told himself. He would be back. With a commitment which only a mountaineer could understand, he was sure that someday he would stand on that colossal peak.

Three times Muir and his friend sailed up and down Puget Sound, entranced by the beautiful "many-fingered hand of the sea." When Magee said good-by at Portland, Muir, boarding another steamer, went north to Alaska.

A group of pompous clergymen and their wives spoiled much of John's pleasure in this trip. With Dr. Jackson, whose speech he had liked in the Yosemite, he had something in common. As for the others, he avoided them. The self-important wives, looking down their noses at him, called him "that wild John Muir."

On July 14th the steamer docked at Wrangell, a rough, lawless Indian town, set in crooked lines along the boggy shore of an island. Up the gangplank came a young man, eager and charming, who greeted each of the missionary party with deference. He was in pleasant contrast to them, Muir thought. At that moment their glances crossed and the newcomer smiled at him.

Suddenly Dr. Jackson included John in the welcome.

"Mr. Muir, this is S. Hall Young, our new missionary to the Stickeen Indians. We are here to brief him on his work. Young, this is Professor Muir, the naturalist."

"And why Professor?" Muir responded with a smile. "Mr. Young, I'm happy to know you!" And Young, feeling oppressed by the solemn men in black, liked at once the tall man in the shabby gray overcoat and Scotch cap, who didn't take himself too seriously.

It was noon of a cloudless day when the river boat, *Cassiar*, dropped anchor at the old Hudson's Bay trading post of Glenora. Already she had steamed for a hundred and fifty miles between huge glaciers and wild canyons, up the rapid Stickeen River. Now she must wait overnight for a favoring wind.

"Amuse yourselves!" the Captain said at lunch. "We'll be here till two o'clock tomorrow morning."

Muir, who had joined the party at Young's request, sent the younger man a glance full of meaning, with just the faintest gesture of his right hand.

"What's on your mind?" Young asked, as they met behind the pilothouse like conspirators.

John pointed to the range of mountains rising abruptly from the shore and to the highest peak, which stood pulpitlike in the center.

"One of the best views in the world."

"How far?"

"Ten miles, perhaps."

"How high?"

"Oh, seven or eight thousand feet."

"I shouldn't go," Young said wistfully. "You know these divines—they keep me in leading strings."

"Eh, mon, are you a child?" Muir answered testily; then he regretted it. " 'Twill be a long, hard climb. I'd best go alone."

"No," said Young, determined now. "I'm a stout walker, and I'm going. I'll send Stickeen Johnny to call all the Indians to a big talk—a *hyou-wawa*. That'll keep the good doctors busy!"

"Well, I have warned you," Muir said. "It's a hard trip —but . . ."

"I can take it!" Young cried.

With the recklessness of youth, he failed to tell John of a weakness which should have prevented his going. It was now twenty minutes past three and days were getting short in this north country. Handing Young two hardtacks for his supper and telling him to "take off his coat," Muir started off briskly. With sure instinct, he chose the easiest way, but from the first it was a tough climb. Fallen trees, hidden by thick brush, trapped them at the beginning. Then came long mountain slopes, sometimes open, but often covered by a solid mass of firs.

After three hours they stood at the edge of a high alpine meadow filled with flowers of every kind and color, from common daisies to tall, nodding campanulas, or the sweet, pink bells of cassiope, the mountain heather. Young was amazed at the joy in John's face. He ran from plant to plant, dropping on his knees to touch them, carefully digging specimens to stuff in his pockets. Meanwhile he chatted to them in a mixture of Scotch baby talk and botanical Latin.

"Well, well, you wee mugginses, how did you stray away from Shasta? Who'd a' thocht to find you here!"

When his own shirtfront and pockets were full of dripping roots and dirt, he tried to turn Young into a walking herbarium. Then he seemed to come to his senses.

"Man, we'll have to hurry, or we'll miss it."

"Miss what?"

"The jewel of the day—sunset from the peak."

Then it seemed to the far younger man beside him that Muir began to *slide* up the mountain with a speed which he had never seen before, though he had climbed with sturdy mountaineers. Only by using every ounce of strength and will power could he keep John in sight. He was breathless; his heart seemed to leap into his throat.

They pushed cautiously across a glacier to the foot of a precipice, which rose, projecting outward, for a good thousand feet above them. How could it be climbed? Young knew he would never have dared it alone. They were in the shadow, but the peaks above them were still in sunlight. Muir attacked the cliff, calling, "Watch out! It's very dangerous here."

Dangerous! The word was hardly needed. Young watched John in astonishment. Such climbing! There was never an instant when both feet and hands were not in play, and often elbows, knees, thighs, upper arms, and even chin must grip and hold. Pulling up smooth rock faces by sheer strength of arm, chinning over the edge, leaping fissures, testing crumbly spurs before risking his weight, always going up, up, no hesitation, no pause—that was Muir.

John climbed so fast that his movements were like flying. Perfect precision, unfailing judgment. Young tried to keep close behind him; to use his footholds, his points of vantage. But the pace was a killing one. Strength seemed to ebb away. He gasped for breath and felt his muscles twitch.

Now the terrible cliff stretched a thousand feet below them. One final effort, they would reach the summit. Muir passed around the shoulder of the highest pinnacle, where the rock was disintegrating, danger of slipping great. "Have a care!" he shouted back, not staying to help, for he felt quite sure of his young friend's skill and strength. Mountain wind carried the words away.

In his haste to overtake Muir, Young tried to leap a sharp-cut fissure, filled with slippery, sliding gravel, which sloped steeply for twelve feet, straight to the edge of the cliff. In the center he saw a rock, the size of a man's head. Surely he could jump to that, then clear the rest! But the stone melted away. He shot with terrible speed down, down toward the precipice. Crying out, whirling on his face, his arms were twisted out of their shoulder sockets and hung useless. He was helpless—sliding, sliding, until his feet hung out over the very edge.

Terrible pain. A wild moment of panic. As if he were drowning, all his past rushed before him. He saw his wife's face, thought of their child about to be born, of his charges, the Indians, who needed him. Then he heard Muir's voice from somewhere above him.

"My God!" came the cry. "Grab that rock, man, just by your right hand!"

Hardly daring to speak, Young struggled to answer. "My arms are out!"

There was a silence. Then the voice came again, calm, firm, undisturbed. "Hold tight! I'll get you out of this. Have to go up and around, cross the rift above, come to you from below. Keep cool!"

Then came whistling and singing, snatches of Scotch songs, slowly receding. The voice was going away. It seemed an endless time. The torture grew worse, but the panic was gone. If anyone could save him, John Muir could. John would come back.

Songs again, gradually coming nearer. "And it's up wi' the Bonnets of Bonnie Dundee!" Then Muir's voice, calm and reassuring, from somewhere below him. "Steady now, I'll have to swing you out over the cliff." Young felt a hand on his back, catching his waistband, shirt, and vest in one firm grip. Suddenly he slid out of the cleft with a shower of gravel. His head swung down and he stared at the glacier a thousand feet below.

"Work downwards with your feet!" John crooked one arm and drew him close. As Young's head came down on Muir's own level, John caught Young's collar with his teeth. Young's iron-shod shoes struck the shelf on which John was standing and soon he was beside him, held by a powerful left arm. For a moment they stopped to breathe, while Muir clung to a projecting knob above them with his right hand.

Then the orders came. "I must let go of you. Need both my hands here. Let your feet climb up the wall!" How it was done perhaps neither man knew, but slowly, carefully, holding Young's collar in his teeth as a panther holds her cubs, Muir managed to climb ten or twelve feet to a broader shelf. Only a moment of safety, Young knew, but in that fleeting instant, hope for life returned and despair left him.

The air was icy; the sun had set. Neither man had a coat and the long, terrible work of the night had just begun. John managed to set one of Young's shoulders, but the other resisted. He strapped the poor, useless arm to Young's side with suspender and handkerchiefs, to keep it from swinging free.

On now, from foothold to foothold. Sometimes Muir packed him on his back; sometimes, going down first, he grasped Young's foot and slowly pulled him downward. It was midnight when they reached the glacier. Skirting the ice plain, coasting down the moraine matter of a long gravel slide like boys on a sled, struggling through a canyon, caught in thickets of willow and alder, the two men fought their way on in the starlight.

When they reached the timber line, Muir stopped to make a fire and let Young rest. Once he tried to persuade him to wait by the fire, while he himself went for help, but Young protested with all his might.

"No, no! I can walk now. Don't leave me!"

Slowly they staggered on, from fire to fire, from rest to rest, until they reached the path to Glenora, then climbed the ship's gangplank in the morning light. Dr. Kendall, one of the men in black, stood barring their way with a frowning face.

"See here, young man, do you know you've kept us waiting? Foolish adventures may do for Muir, but you have work to do—family, a church, no right to risk your life!"

But Nat Lane, the captain of the *Cassiar*, elbowed the minister aside. "Blast it! Must you always preach? Can't you see the man's bad hurt? Out of the way, sir!"

All his life S. Hall Young felt grateful to Muir, who never blamed him for having brought both of them to the edge of death. In his pride he had concealed the fact that he had once been crippled by a horse that fell with him, leaving him with weakened arms and shoulders. He was, as he had boasted, a "stout walker," but he would never try mountain climbing again.

Through the summer and fall Muir stayed on in Southeastern Alaska. Often he longed for Louie, to see her face, to take her in his arms. But already he had complete faith in her integrity. She wouldn't wish him to return if his work was unfinished. Though he had made Young's home his, from the time of their wild climb together, he was rarely there. With friends or alone, he explored the ranges, forests, and inland lakes, going thirty miles upriver to the hot springs, or visiting the "mud glacier."

During the summer wet season, the time of the *Soonah,* or southeast rain-wind, Muir sometimes stayed indoors working on notes and pencil sketches. He was also waiting for Young, who, in turn, was waiting the advent of a small new member of the family. Through the quiet days the two men planned a trip with all the gusto of boys. Almost all of the Alexandrian Archipelago, that vast network of 1100 islands forming the cup handle of Alaska, was unexplored. Young wished to visit and number the tribes of the Thlinget Indians to the North and West. John was eager to study mountains and forests, but especially glaciers, those huge, moving rivers of ice which made all that he had seen before seem pygmies. Most important of all, they might modify, or add to, his knowledge of early glacial action in the Sierra.

As he wandered about Fort Wrangell, talking with white men and Indians, he heard of a mysterious inland bay, where the greatest glaciers stood. It was not on the chart, the only one, made by Vancouver in 1807. But yes, it was real, the Indians said. No white man had ever seen it.

Should he stay on in Alaska? This was the answer. To find an unknown, unmapped bay was the one sure incentive John Muir needed.

By October poor Louie Strenzel had almost forgotten her promise "never to interfere with John's work." Letters were few and far between. She was lonely and anxious. It was not enough to read his vivid tales of Alaska in the *San Francisco Bulletin*, though she was proud of these. Everyone was talking about them. Even the big Eastern newspapers were copying them and the *Bulletin* had doubled its circulation.

One day Louie's resistance broke. She wrote John a letter which was a cry of distress. "So far, so far away . . . and still another month of wandering in that wild Northland . . . I shiver with every thought of the dark, cruel winter drifting down, down. What a blessed Thanksgiving, if only you come home!"

Poor Louie! Did she have some dim foreboding of what it might mean to be an explorer's wife in the years ahead? At least, there was no weakening of her love for him. About the time Louie wrote, John was sending a very different message. On October 9th he said, "I am just beginning to discover my real work," and added several days later, "Leaving for the North in a few minutes. The Indians are waiting. Farewell!"

From the first Muir had found himself in sympathy with these Indians of the north coast, so unlike the forbidding specimens he had seen in Nevada or the Yosemite. He liked their willingness to work, their skill with tools, their natural dignity, the gentleness with which they treated their children. Children rarely cried and were never scolded.

In turn, the Indians gave to Muir liking and respect. A man of their own kind, at one with nature, wise in woodcraft, walking serenely and at peace with the Great Spirit, finding Him, as they did, in stones, trees, or mountain peaks. They listened to him with reverence.

To John's vast amazement, he was made a member of the Stickeen tribe. Now he had an Indian name—*Ancoutahan*, Adopted Chief. It was given to him in high ceremony at a feast, in honor of the "Great Visiting Doctors," along with the fantastic headdress of a medicine man. Though at first he took his tribal membership far from seriously, he was soon corrected by Young. "You are safe now anywhere in Alaska," he told John. "An Indian name protects you. Without it you might be robbed or killed, but no strange tribe will touch you, knowing you are a Stickeen, that they will take vengeance."

Muir and Young stood waiting at the wharf in Wrangell beside the six-fathom canoe of cedar, their passport to adventure. Chief Toyatte, owner and captain, watched closely as the luggage was stowed—blankets, extra clothes, provisions. Guns, fishhooks, spears, and clam sticks would have to add to the meager supply of flour, beans, bacon, sugar, salt, and dried fruit. The crew of three, Kodachan, John the interpreter, and Sitka Charley, moved quickly and well.

At last they were in their places. Toyatte's paddle flashed in the sun. Down the steps from the wharf to the canoe came a grim figure, Kodachan's mother, who stood gazing at Young in silence. "Wait!" she shrilled, bursting into angry predictions. "You are going into danger among

evil tribes, into bloodshed and storms. If my son does not
return, on you will be his blood and you shall pay. I
say it!"

Though Young answered soothingly, the woman stood
there hostile and unmoved. The four Indians seemed
troubled as they pushed off and Toyatte, also, added his
tale of woe. His wife had refused to say good-by, had
wept and predicted his death. But soon, with every shining mile of Sumner Strait, with every flash of the paddle,
with Muir's questions and Young's cheerful answers, the
first ominous mood fled away.

Two weeks' sailing brought them to Icy Strait and the
main village of the Hoonahs. The men of this tribe were
seal hunters and wide ranging. Yes, they knew the bay
John sought. It was called Sitadakay and had ice mountains, but no gold. That night, as they all hugged the fire,
they tried their best to warn him away from it. Koosta-
Kah, the awful otter-man, lived there. He seized sleeping
campers and hung them up in the tops of trees. There was
a killer whale, and in one long arm of the bay a giant
devilfish that dragged men down and mangled them.

Sensing the fear of his own Indians, John hired one of
the Hoonahs to go as guide. Later he picked up a load
of firewood, since no tree, bush, or blade of grass, they
said, could grow on the shores. It was a harsh day, with
cold pelting rain; wind bitter, but in their favor, as they
sailed up the southwest side of the bay into a land of rock
and ice. Through shifting mists they saw the great blue
cliffs of the first glacier, terrifying in its savage power.

The roar of newborn icebergs, breaking from the cliffs, thundering into the bay, met and answered the roar of the storm.

An hour and a half beyond the glacier, they ran into a harbor with a low shore, where the canoe could be pulled up, safe from drifting bergs. Here the guide said they must camp for the night. Muir protested, since it was early, but the others sided against him. Trying to rest on the bare granite, they listened all night long to "the bombardment of the ice-guns." The next day was Sunday and Young refused to stir.

Muir started out alone, glad to use his legs again after sitting hour on hour, cramped and wet, in a canoe. But it was hard going. He pushed on through rain and mud, crossing brown torrents, choked with rocks, wallowing in snow up to his armpits, till at last he reached a ridge over a thousand feet high. As the mists parted, he caught a glimpse of the second enormous glacier, vast and impressive beyond him. Then the clouds lifted further. He saw the berg-filled bay, the huge mountains about it, the "solitude of ice and snow and newborn rocks." As he stood fighting the wind, leaning against it, he managed to count five great glaciers and tried with numbed fingers to sketch the terrain in his notebook.

All day he wandered, reaching camp by dark. He had crossed avalanche slopes and treacherous torrents, he had fought the wind and the snow; he was chilled to the bone and half starved, but in his heart burned a flame of excitement which nothing could quench. He was the first white man to penetrate the loneliness, to learn the secrets of the wild "Unknown Bay."

That night John found the crew sullen and hostile. The Hoonah guide had taken sides with the Stickeen Indians. No, he would lead them no further. It was dangerous now to go close to the glaciers. Too late in the season, the weather too bad. If he took them to the end of the bay, the bergs would close in and trap them. They would all die, as many of his own tribe had done. Even brave old Chief Toyatte said his "heart was bad," he could stand the strain no longer.

John, rising, stood and looked solemnly at each of the Indians in turn; then he spoke. He told them that for ten years he had wandered alone over the mountains in storms and snows, and good luck always followed him. With John Muir they need fear nothing. Soon the sun would shine again. The Great Spirit would care for them, as long as they were trustful and brave. Therefore, they must put away all childish fear.

For a long while there was silence; then Chief Toyatte rose and stood beside him. "Your talk was good," he said. "Now my heart is strong again. I will venture with John Muir as long and as far as he wills. Even if the canoe is broken and I go to the other world, I shall not greatly care. I shall go with a good companion."

Returning down the bay, after five days of exploration, they found the biggest glacier of all. It was a mile and a half wide; the face of it rose from four to seven hundred feet above the water. Masses of ice, breaking off and falling from a height, made waves so huge that landing was impossible. Later it was named the Muir Glacier, a fitting tribute to its discoverer.

In spite of the snow, John persuaded the men to turn into Sum Dum Bay and paddle up its southeastern arm. Now the ice pack began to close in, the Indians refused to go further. John, who was sure that another immense glacier must stand at the end of the fiord, was deeply disappointed. Old Toyatte remarked firmly, "Big Sum Dum ice mountain hides his face."

The expedition left its last camp November twenty-first at daybreak, weather calm and bright. Wrangell Island came into view beneath a rosy sky, all the forest down to the water's edge silvery-gray with a sprinkling of snow. Back at last!

On April 14th, 1880, almost a year after he left for the North, John and Louie stood up to be married in the little white house at Martinez. Perhaps it was divine justice, since John had so often praised storms, that the day was a horrible one, the minister delayed by floods, guests forced to arrive in stained, wet clothes.

But inside the house it was all fair weather. The walls were decorated with apple blossoms; music flowed through the rooms; gayety and happiness were everywhere. Mrs. Carr wrote from her home in the South that Louie was the "one woman" she would have chosen for her friend, John Muir.

John was happy, fortunate in his wife, liking her parents, who were also his friends. They moved out of the house in which the wedding was held, giving it to their children as a present, with twenty acres of land planted to orchards and vineyards. True, Mrs. Strenzel wrote in her diary that she had hoped they might all live together, but Dr. Strenzel was wiser. He knew that young people needed to build their lives alone and he rejoiced that now he could have the bigger, finer house which he had wanted.

It was a wonderful spring. Roses and ivy climbed together over the pillars of the wide porch, the air was murmurous with the hum of bees. The little house stood high, looking with its clear windows across rolling hills and orchards on to the shining waters of Carquinez Straits.

In the night, safe in the warmth of Louie's arms, John found the deepest fulfillment he had ever known. And yet, sometimes, as she slept and he lay staring into the darkness, he dreamed a waking dream of the wild North Country and of the lost glacier he had failed to find.

11

The Rope of Ice

SHORTLY AFTER HIS MARRIAGE, JOHN BEGAN TO WORK ON the land with an enthusiasm which seemed strange to him. Twenty beautiful acres now belonged to them both; from them he could earn a competence for his wife and the children they hoped for. Competence? Yes, even more, he boasted inwardly.

It was plain that Dr. Strenzel had won wealth and success. He had been the first fruit grower in California to import European stock and plant fine table grapes—Tokay, Muscat, Cornichan, and Emperor. They stretched over a hundred acres, glistening ribbons of green.

John set himself to absorb all the advice he could from his father-in-law. He went into the fields and worked with Chinese laborers, early and late. The sharp click of the pruning shears became familiar music. By July the hardest of the toil was over; the early digging, pruning, spraying, tying, and training of the vines was mainly past. In October would come the harvest. He must learn techniques of picking and marketing then. Yes, he should be on hand for that! But the period in between, while the sun was doing its ripening—would this give him some freedom for his own real work?

An urgent letter came from his friend, Thomas Magee, who was leaving for an Alaskan trip. Would John share it? Would he indeed? But could he, that was the question! Talking it over with Louie in their room at night, he was conscious of her disappointment. "I had hoped," she said slowly and then added quickly, "No, I was never to say that! Of course you must go if you wish it."

After all, she would be safe at home, with parents near and old Martinez friends close by. It was not like leaving her alone. Stifling his qualms, John sailed for the North on the last day of July.

To S. Hall Young, standing at the dock with all the rest of Fort Wrangell's population to see the mail steamer come in, it seemed that time had shot suddenly backward. There, standing on the deck in just the same spot was the same tall man, in the same old gray ulster and Scotch cap, he had seen the year before. Then the tall man waved and shouted. Springing ashore, he cried, "When can you be ready?"

"Muir!" Young answered, with a warm and eager hand-clasp. "What does this mean? Thought you were just married. Where's your wife?"

"Eh, mon, have you forgotten? We lost a glacier last fall. Wife couldn't come, so I've come alone. There's no time to lose. Get your canoe and crew together and let's be off!"

Briefly John went on to Sitka. When he came back, he found that Young was waiting and ready. To his great distress, brave old Chief Toyatte, who had led them before, was dead, the tragic victim of a brawling enemy tribe. Captain Lot Tyeen took his place with his son-in-law, Joe, and Billy, the half-breed interpreter. They were a good crew, young, alert, and powerful.

No predictions of disaster spoiled this calm midsummer day when the twenty-five-foot canoe lay at the Wrangell wharf. But Muir and Young were keeping it waiting as they stood on the pier, lost in argument.

"I say no!" John cried gruffly. "What is he but a helpless wisp of fur? An infernal nuisance, that's what he'll be! Send one of the Indians back with him, if he hasn't the sense . . ."

"You don't know Stickeen," Young kept saying hotly. "He always goes with me. Never makes trouble, never yelps, whines, begs, or steals or gets in the way."

"Then he isn't a dog," said John, "and we don't want him!"

The object of his wrath waited patiently—a small black, tan-and-white, long-haired cur with an air of indifference. Now and then he blinked sleepily and his fringed tail seemed to droop. At last, while the discussion raged, he turned, walked calmly down the gangplank into the canoe, found the bow, turned round three times, and lay down on his master's coat. Here he dropped his narrow pointed nose on two front paws and closed his eyes.

Suddenly Young burst into a roar of laughter and John

looked sheepishly back at him, accepting defeat at the paws of a little cur who knew what he wanted.

"*Ut-hah, ut-hah!* Pull, Pull!" Joe and Billy cried, rising from their seats with every stroke of the long oars, as the canoe leapt forward. In the high stern behind them, Captain Tyeen wielded his big steering blade. Toward the bow, back of the mast, Young and Muir sat with paddles ready. A day of days, John thought, as the gleaming water creamed along the sides of the canoe. The sky was a savage blue, the lower hills ringed with white clouds, while far above them, the great peaks shone in dazzling ice and snow, marching like a triumphant army toward the North.

Now and then John sent a sceptical glance down at the sleeping dog, who had so barely escaped being left behind. How little he knew that this member of the expedition would prove in the end to be its master!

On through tortuous Wrangell Narrows and on past bold Point Windham! As they headed toward Sum Dum Bay, John urged the Indians to speed. This must be a swift trip, without delays at villages or speeches to tribes. He must return on the October boat. With every shining mile he grew more anxious about Louie, troubled by a premonition that she was ill and needed him. Telling himself that this was due to his regret at leaving her, he tried to shrug away his worries—in vain.

Five days brought them to Sum Dum Bay, with its three gigantic arms. Here they had started to explore the year before, but the ice pack and the Indians' fear of it had driven them out. Could they find it now, the lost glacier of which he had dreamed?

They crossed the bay and on August twenty-first started up the western, or right-hand, fiord. Not on Vancouver's map. No white man had ever invaded this sleeping world. Mile on mile they pushed their way on, through cruising icebergs, between stupendous cliffs. By seven o'clock at night they came to what seemed to be the end—but there was no glacier.

Then one of the Indians shouted and pointed with his paddle. A narrow opening, leading sharply to the right between towering granite walls, swallowed up the canoe. They crept closely along one side, fighting against a great rush of wind and tide and charging bergs. The light grew dimmer. Was night overtaking them in this narrow canyon, trapping them beyond return? But a bend in the "wild yosemite" gave Muir his first sight of the great glacier which had been so desperately hidden, "pouring its deep, broad flood into the fiord, while berg after berg broke from it with thunderous uproar."

"Hah!" cried the Indians, joining in Muir's shout of triumph. "There is your lost friend. He says *sagh-a-ya*, how do you do! He fires his biggest guns in your honor."

Gradually John's first dislike of Stickeen faded away. He was not a nuisance; did not yelp, fuss, whine, or get in the way, or prove unruly in the canoe. He was unemotional as a glacier; never a tail wag, even if a friendly hand patted his small, black head. He seemed to John "a dim, dull, unromantic nobody, as unfussy as a tree." But two things interested Muir—the little dog's deep, intelligent, always watchful eyes and the fact that he seemed to sense a landing, even before the crew was alerted. Not a word was spoken nor had the boat turned toward shore, when Stickeen would rouse himself, crawl toward the bow, leap, and stand upon the high prow, poised like a small figurehead. He was the first ashore, even if he had to swim for it. Once there, he went gravely about his business, usually something to do with field mice or pine squirrels.

Day by day, the little dog tried to win Muir's favor. Though he had been Young's puppy from the beginning, carried in his pocket when he was only a ball of fur, if the two men separated it was John whom he followed. Into John's tent he crawled at night, to sleep curled up at his feet. He often refused to eat if John would not feed him. To Young's amusement, John said at last, "There's more in that wee beastie than I thought."

There came a day of torrential rain. For many miles they had been buffeted by head winds and tidal waves, as they crept along at the foot of dizzying cliffs. They were nearing the open Pacific and the *Soonah*, or southeast rain-wind, was howling through the entrance to Cross Sound. They fought their way around a point and entered the welcome harbor of Taylor Bay. Sliding into a sheltered cove, they beached the canoe and made camp as best they could, with sodden blankets and soaking tents. In spite of the driving rain, the two men went for a tour of observation.

"Here's something new," cried Muir, as they stood at the foot of a towering glacier.

"What's new?" asked Young.

"All other glaciers in this region are receding, but this one's coming forward. Do you see the crushed and splintered forests at its sides and front? The ice plow is at work. I must explore here tomorrow."

"Wish I could go with you," said Young wistfully. "But I shall never forget Glenora Peak."

"Nor I!" answered Muir.

Early the next morning the wind was still howling and the rain drifting in sheets. Young knew that a living, moving glacier, beaten and swept by storm, would mean only high drama and joy to John Muir. Then he caught the older man stirring. Though half asleep, he heard his voice in the darkness.

"Go back, you stupid, wilful little muggins! Go back, I say. Lie down!"

The dog against the man. Which one would win? Thinking he knew, Young slid down again into dreams.

Not wishing to rouse the camp, Muir wolfed a swift breakfast of bread and rain and ran out into the gale. Turning to catch his breath, he saw Stickeen coming after him, boring through the storm.

"Go back!" He shouted once more, stamping his foot and pointing. "I can't carry or help you. This is no day

for you. Go back." But the little dog stood his ground with
lowered head and blinking eyes. When John went on he
followed, with his curious foxlike glide. At last Muir
gave up, told him to come on, and gave him the crust he
had in his pocket.

As they pushed up through a ragged edge of woods
to the east side of the glacier, the storm seemed to grow
worse. John took shelter back of a tree and waited, while
Stickeen stood at his feet. But at last the rain seemed to
lessen. Pulling off his heavy rubber boots and overcoat,
Muir left them on a log where he could find them later.
Anyway he would be soaked to the skin! Why carry an
extra load? Then he retied his mountain shoes, tightened
his belt, shouldered his ice axe, and so, free and ready for
rough work, he pushed on, ignoring the rain.

Someway he felt lost and lonely in the low, dragging
mist. Only a prairie of ice in sight now; moaning of the
wind or the rattle of falling stones the only sound. A
sense of danger haunted him, as if coming events were
casting ominous shadows. But Stickeen, undisturbed and
stalwart, followed calmly at his heels.

After two hours of hard work, Muir came to a maze
of crevasses, deep and difficult to cross. But, as always,
his nerves seemed firmed by danger. Cutting careful footholds to give him a stance, he managed wide leaps across
them, while Stickeen soared over like a bird.

At last, to his dismay, John found himself on the edge
of the widest chasm he had yet discovered, forty or fifty
feet wide, he thought, and terribly deep. Slowly he traced

the edge north and south, only to realize that he was on an island of ice, caught as in a deathtrap. Kneeling down and gazing into the depths of the awful crevasse, he saw what seemed to be the only means of escape—a long sliver of ice which stretched, like a drooping rope, from one side to the other. But the end of it was ten feet below the glacier's edge, and to climb up on the other side seemed hopeless.

Digging a place at the edge of the glacier for his knees to rest in, he began to cut steps down the smooth ice wall of the chasm. Now Stickeen came up behind him, put his head over John's shoulder, looked, and turned away with a low, pitiful whine. Then he ran searching along the edge, only to come back yelping dismally.

John, who had never seen the little dog lose courage before, was amazed at his instant awareness of danger. Step by step now, Muir inched his way down to the end of the sliver. "Death seemed to lie brooding in the gloom of the chasm." He leaned forward, got astride of it, shaved smooth the top of the drooping ice rope in front of him to make a path for Stickeen. Slowly, slowly, lest the thin line of safety break, he hitched himself forward. Never once did he glance down on either hand—the ice-blue sliver was his entire world.

A space of time, terrible and endless. He reached the opposite side, rose cautiously to his feet, and called to the frightened little dog, who was crying as if his heart would break, "Come, Stickeen! You must come to me. Come, Stickeen!"

And Stickeen, who trusted him even to the edge of death, "hushed his screaming fears," worked his small paws down from notch to notch and, holding steady against the gusty wind, crawled slowly across the dreadful, slanting bridge to reach the other side. John cut notches and fingerholds in the wall before him, climbed—and escaped. He leaned down to help Stickeen, but, sure of himself now, he quickly hooked his feet into the steps of the icy wall and bounded up in a rush.

Round and round in crazy whirls of joy, rolling over and over, jumping against John's face, the "little dog-child, Stickeen," celebrated his own deliverance. "Saved!" he seemed to bark ecstatically over and over again. "Saved, saved, saved!"

"And so, the Lord loving us both, we got back to camp. He was indeed a fellow-creature, a little boy in distress in the guise of a dog."

Of all the things that happened to John Muir on his second Alaskan voyage the most meaningful was his experience with Stickeen. More important than the discovery of a glacier, or the mapping of an unknown fiord, was this glimpse deep into the heart of a "child-dog of the wilderness."

"Simply by pronouncing the one fetish word *instinct*, all the mental powers of animals lose their significance . . . but Stickeen had in him a little of everything that is in man. He had his share of hopes, fears, joys, griefs, imagination, memory, soul as well as body. He was a horizontal man-child, his heart beating in accord with the universal heart of nature."

Down through the years John Muir told the story of brave Stickeen to groups of children in parlors or by campfires, to friends who asked for it, to big audiences in packed lecture halls. Seventeen years later he immortalized him in a book, thereby making him one of the best loved dogs in all literature.

Years afterward, S. Hall Young also turned his memories into a book, called "Alaska Days with John Muir." "Nearly all of our days were cold, wet and uncomfortable," he wrote, "but of all these so-called hardships Muir made nothing and I caught his spirit. Therefore the beauty, the glory, the wonder, and the thrills of those weeks of exploration are with me yet—a rustless, inexhaustible treasure."

When John reached Sitka on his homeward way, he found a bundle of mail. But alas, the news was not all good. On top of the pile was a letter from Dr. Strenzel, making real his shadowy fears. Louie had had a serious fall and been for many days in fever and pain, but she would not let him try to reach her husband. "I gave him his freedom," she said. "Would you make me break my word?"

Down in the bundle was a much later letter from Louie herself. She wrote she had had "many sleepless nights of strange shadows . . . and wild phantoms," but that she was almost well again. "I know now that neither time nor

space can ever separate us and that wherever you are—
here or there—I am truly with you."

Poor Louie! She was indeed, as Mrs. Carr had said,
"the one woman for John Muir," staunch descendant of
intrepid pioneers. She little knew how far and how harshly
the future might test her.

"What a blessed Thanksgiving, if only you were here,"
Louie had written wistfully the year before, though, as
she wrote it, John was already pushing on further north.
But this year he was back in time. "A wonderful day,"
Mrs. Strenzel confided happily to her diary. She was so
grateful she could hardly eat! She had meant to fill the
house with guests, but it seemed a sacrilege to break the
family circle, now that "Mr. Muir" was home. (She called
him Mr. Muir in true Victorian dignity. Perhaps, too, it
was a sign of respect.)

A cold, gray day outside, with California sun in hiding.
Inside, warmth and light and happiness. Delicious odors
stole from the kitchen—of turkey roasting in its own juice,
of little white onions cooked in cream, of mince pies, hot
with brandy.

The dinner table was festive with flowers and ferns,
great bowls of fruit, nuts and jellies and homemade wine.
Mrs. Strenzel swept to her place, her long black silk rustling across the floor, her crisp, white cap nodding. There
were red rosebuds in Louie's dark hair. At the end of the
dinner came a huge plum pudding, set in a circle of flame.

Love and mutual respect and gratitude—it was indeed

a powerful circle holding them together, shutting them in. Was it possible that Muir, the wanderer, who had just the other day wolfed "bread and rain" for breakfast or fried porpoise meat at night, wondered for one flickering moment whether he belonged here at all?

It was a good winter that year. John worked hard on the land, renting additional acres from his father-in-law. Louie seemed to grow happier and lovelier with each passing day, eagerly anticipating the birth of her baby. In December John wrote to his oldest sister, Margaret, "We expect a visit soon from a relative of the family who has no name as yet."

It was March twenty-sixth and all the morning long he had been fitfully tramping up and down his room, not liking to leave the house, finding it impossible to work. Louie, his beloved Louie, must face this struggle alone. At two o'clock there came a knock on his door. Throwing it wide, he found Mrs. Strenzel standing there, with a wriggling pink flannel bundle in her arms.

"See what I've brought you!" she cried. "Your own new little daughter!"

"Louie?" John asked, with lips dry and voice trembling, though one glance at the old lady's beaming face should have satisfied him.

"Resting now. You may see her soon. Put out your arms, son!" (All the formality was gone.)

Hungrily John took the small, twisting form and held it close to his heart. He peered down at a little red face with a convincing dome of soft, brown fuzz above it.

"Beautiful!" he murmured, unashamed of the tears in his eyes. "Isn't she beautiful, Mother Strenzel?"

"Yes," said the old lady briskly, "just as beautiful as she can be, John."

The month after Annie Wanda's arrival was a wonderful time for Louie and John, for they knew a happiness beyond all their early dreams. Her father's first statement was true. Wanda was a perfect baby, healthy and good, growing in strength and beauty every day.

"I am so glad that you have found there is some happiness outside of glaciers," a friend wrote to John and with all his heart he answered, "Amen." How could he ever leave his home again? It was just as well that they had this breathing space, for only a month later the blow fell. This was still John Muir, the explorer, the man of action, always ready to heed the call to adventure.

All over the world at this time there was a rising interest in polar expeditions, for the North Pole still remained the great undiscovered lure and mystery, the eternal challenge to the stouthearted. Two years before, an American naval officer, George Washington De Long, with thirty-three men and a three-master barque, the *Jeanette*, had set out for the Pole—and vanished.

As the months grew into years, a wave of indignation swept the country, demand for a searching party to find and rescue the lost. Petitions poured into Congress. When the American Geographical Society appealed to President Garfield, there was action at last.

One day, almost a month after the birth of his child, John came into the house, carrying the usual bundle of mail. In it he had found a disturbing letter. How could he ever share its contents with Louie? The letter was franked, and contained what was almost a command invitation to join the officers of the steamer, *Corwin*, soon to be sent to the Arctic in search of De Long.

Captain Calvin L. Hooper, in command of the staunch Revenue steamer, was an old friend of John's. He knew Muir well as a man distinguished for glacial studies and for his mapping of unknown parts of the Alaskan coast. He also knew him as a man among men, strong, intrepid, and used to hardship. He was determined to have him in his party. Muir's decision must be immediate. Already, on April 29th, Captain Hooper was being given a farewell dinner in Oakland. When John broke his news to the Strenzels, they were horrified.

"Leave your wife and child now?" Dr. Strenzel cried. "It's incredible!"

"Then I'll refuse," John answered gently and they thought the matter closed. But later, much disturbed, Louie brought up the question again.

"John, why do you wish to join this expedition?"

"Did I say so?"

"No, but I understand."

"Well . . ." John spoke haltingly. "I have a fellow feeling for those poor duffers caught somewhere up in the vicious ice pack. I'd like to help."

"Yes, of course! You would! What else does it mean to you?"

"Didn't I tell you once that I wished to visit the islands in Bering Sea to study their glacial action, to compare it with Southern Alaska? Didn't I say that I longed to visit the Arctic? And here," cried John with growing excitement, "is my one great chance!"

"A dangerous chance?"

"Yes—I'll not deny that—yes."

"John, you haven't seemed so very well lately. You've worked too hard in the sun, you've slaved morning and night. You're dreadfully thin. I haven't liked your coughing."

"It's nothing."

"The North, away from this low, hot climate, might help you?"

"Perhaps. But I don't want to leave you now, Louie."

"I think that's nonsense," said Louie. "I'm well again and the baby's the pink of perfection. I say you're to go if you wish—I say you're to go!"

12

Fight for
the Forests

ON THE FOURTH OF MAY THE STEAMER *Thomas Corwin*
sailed out of San Francisco Bay to the sound of cannon,
whistles from smaller craft, the dipping of flags and im-
promptu salutes. As he watched from the deck, Muir
could not help remembering that to just such fanfare the
Jeanette had sailed two years before.

For many weeks the stout little vessel followed the
coast of Alaska or zigzagged across to the bleak Siberian
shore. Everywhere the men in charge tried desperately
to find news or trace of the lost De Long. To this John
gave his best wisdom and knowledge of Alaskan waters.

Now they played hide and seek with the cruel ice pack,
interviewed Eskimos, rode out a gale, or struggled with
a broken rudder. Opposite Koliuchin Island they landed
a searching party which followed the Siberian coast westward. Twenty-seven days later, picked up by the returning *Corwin*, they made their report. They had learned
absolutely nothing.

By the middle of August they managed to gain the

southeast cape of Wrangell Land, that mysterious country the dimensions of which no man then knew, the soil of which no white man had ever trod. With throttle wide, they forced their way to shore through grinding ice blocks.

While Hooper and Muir explored, officers of the *Corwin* built a cairn, left records, and set the United States flag on a bluff, facing the sea. Though they looked carefully for burned-out fires, footprints, cairns, or any sign of De Long, the result again was—failure. John, who would gladly have given his life for the missing men, for one mad moment wished to be left behind to explore alone. That it was impossible madness the Captain firmly assured him.

It was the beginning of fall when the *San Francisco Bulletin* published Muir's tragic statement from Point Barrow; "We have found no trace of the lost *Jeanette*." On October twenty-first, the day when Muir reached home, De Long and the few men left with him were still fighting cold, despair, starvation on the barren Siberian shore.

Five and a half months from the time he started John Muir returned, hearty and well, with eyes bluer than ever in a face burned black by the Arctic sun. He soon plunged into work, writing the whole story for the press, sorting out plants destined for Asa Gray and Harvard, working on his government report.

The news of the *Jeanette's* disaster reached a shocked world on December twenty-first, but it was spring of the following year before the death of De Long and his men was definitely known. Often after his return and even oftener after the tragic news came, Louie noticed a sadness in John's face, a brooding look in his eyes. Understanding, asking no questions, she slipped a hand into his. One day he turned to her and said quietly, "I can't forget, or forgive myself. We should have found them."

"You tried—in every way you knew!" said Louie.

Soon after Muir's return from the *Corwin* cruise, he was called upon by Senator Miller of California to help draw up two bills to be introduced in Congress. The first provided for the enlargement of the Yosemite Valley and Mariposa Grove grants, and the second was concerned with setting aside a new tract of land as a park.

Alas for all the hours spent in consultation and map drawing! Both bills died in the Public Lands Committee without reaching the Senate, since the good men in power found the measures "extreme" and "impossible." Lawmakers in the year 1881 were many of them tools of the lumber, mining, or railroad interests.

Keenly aware of the attitudes of this period, Sigurd F. Olson, the former president of the National Parks Association, has written in his book, "Listening Point," "We forget that then men thought of the wilderness as something to be eliminated, that forests existed only to be cut. No one had ever heard of recreational values or conservation of natural resources. The pine stands were thought inexhaustible and no one could have imagined a day might come when trees had other values than lumber. It was inevitable that most of the great forests should disappear and that today there are only a few places where they can still be found."

"No one had ever heard of conservation." In the main, true. But John Muir had dreamed of it and Increase Lapham had preached it even before the Civil War. He had gone from one end of Wisconsin to the other, warning people against the coming exhaustion of the forests. And John had known of him in his years at Madison. "Saving a bit of pure wildness" was a favorite idea of John's from the days when he was young. Sloping down on the north side of Fountain Lake, just below the house where he grew up, was a meadow full of flowers—lady-slippers, fragrant arethusas, and grass pinks; later, asters and goldenrod and tall bullrushes. John loved the place. He asked Dave Galloway, Sarah's husband, to fence and save it. But Dave had called this foolish. "The fence would be broken; it would be useless."

When Galloway sold the land to Sam Ennis, John tried again. It was the time of his first California job. "Ask whatever price you wish," he wrote to Ennis, "but sell me the land." This appeal failed. But here was the germ of an idea which afterwards grew into the plan for national parks, a plan to save the unusual places of our country as monuments, not to be changed or destroyed, to be kept safe in their beauty forever.

Disheartened by the failure of the bills, John turned to his own affairs. The growing dependence of Dr. Strenzel gave him added care. The ranch and his family needed him; he set himself to meet these needs. His own tastes would always be simple, but he must earn money for his family. With a Scotch doggedness, he dropped his public career and devoted himself to fruit raising. Many of his friends considered these to be wasted years.

More practical than his father-in-law, John gave up growing grain and replanted that land with grapes and fruit trees. Where Dr. Strenzel had grown many varieties of fruit, Muir, finding Tokay grapes and Bartlett pears sold best, regrafted much of the stock to popular varieties.

Muir's shrewdness, his success and ability to deal with men, became a legend. Ranch wagons rumbled down Alhambra Valley at dawn, carting fruit to the Strenzel wharf; buyers swarmed off the first river boat. Once the men formed a combine, agreeing not to meet Muir's price till they forced it down.

"Take our bid or your fruit will rot!"

"Let it rot!" John answered with a grin.

The next steamer bought up the fruit at his own price.

Early rising was the habit of a lifetime to John. He was first at the station in the morning, after the railroad had come through, waiting to claim his quota of crates shipped back by city dealers. Since he was early, he managed to choose strong, undamaged boxes.

Now he reverted again to his old love of inventions and devised gadgets to speed up the work. Mrs. Strenzel, who never missed a detail, noted in her diary how the labor was helped by a machine for each man, which let him plant the vines straight, quickly, with less effort.

"He has a green thumb," Martinez neighbors said of John and often thought (with no little malice) he had the fingers of Midas as well. It was a common sight to see him drive up to the Martinez bank, pull a fat white laundry bag that clinked out of the buggy and vanish inside. The Strenzel products had always been favorites, but John's expert management doubled demand and profits, till the balance seemed to grow of itself in the village savings account. At the end of this ranching period, fifty thousand dollars stood at interest, never touched in his lifetime; and big balances lay hidden in San Francisco banks.

"I had more money," John wrote in his memoirs, "than I thought I would ever need for my family, or for any expense of travel or study, no matter how long continued."

If wealth had brought happiness, this would have been the climax of the years for John Muir. But here was a man to whom the touchstone of life had been freedom. Conflict with his father, memories of a childhood made harsh by drudgery, had left him with a hatred for routine toil. This was too close to the old, bitter pattern.

At the end of January, 1886, another little girl was born to the Muirs, a bewitching baby with big, appealing eyes and light brown curls, but lacking the vigor of her older sister. From the first her father and mother were anxious about Helen, or Midge, as John lovingly called her. Louie would not take her from the ranch or leave her behind, and John would not wander away from his family, no matter how much he longed for mountain air or a taste of the old freedom.

Now, as his father-in-law grew feebler, the work of two ranches began to fall on his shoulders. He was on a treadmill, overburdened and driven. In spite of himself, he dreamed of long, timeless days in the wilderness, of mountain peaks still unexplored.

Louie was disturbed, as she saw her husband grow thin, pale, and weary, with the racking cough which was a danger signal. This further trouble doubled her worry about little Helen. Others, also, were anxious about John Muir, editors like Robert Underwood Johnson or Sam Williams of the *San Francisco Bulletin*. They turned to him for material and met only a brusque refusal. Still others, who had read his articles with enthusiasm and looked to him for leadership in the fight for the forests, felt themselves let down—deserted. Why had John Muir dropped out of the world?

One day, toward the end of this strange, seven-year interval, S. Hall Young, his friend of Alaska days, appeared at the Martinez ranch. He was unexpected and found Muir out in the cherry orchard, superintending his men.

"Ah, my friend!" John cried, dropping his basket and rushing forward with outstretched hands, "I have been longing mightily for you! You have come to take me on a canoe trip to the countries beyond? My weariness of this humdrum life has grown so heavy that it is like to crush me. I'm ready to go with you, whenever you say."

"No," Young answered, "I'm leaving Alaska."

"Man, man," Muir cried, "how can you do it? Look at me and take warning. I who have lived a life of freedom, condemned to penal servitude with these miserable little baldheads—and for money. Man, I'd like to die for the shame of it!"

At the end John lapsed into broad Scotch, as he always did in moments of stress. "Gin it were na' for my bairnies, I'd run awa' from a' this tribble an' haul ye back north wi' me!"

Young spent the night and talked with John for most of it. When he left he was sadly troubled. For days afterward Muir's lament rang in his ears. *"I'm learning nothing here that will do me any good."*

It was true that a few breaks came to add variety to John's life, but not always happy ones. One August day he was reading in his study. Suddenly he dropped his book and sat staring into space. An inner voice seemed to speak to him. "Go east at once; your father is dying."

There had been no word that the old man was ill. Crippled for ten years, he had been living with his youngest daughter, Joanna, in Kansas City. John had not seen him for over eighteen years, though he had often sent money for his care. Where the voice came from Muir did not know, but it was a summons, a command. It never occurred to him to question it.

Reaching Portage by train, he tried to persuade his mother to join him, but Anne was too old and tired.

Davie pleaded his work; he hated to leave the store. When
John bought a train ticket for him, he decided to go. At
Lincoln, Nebraska, Danny, a busy doctor, dropped his
practice, since John's certainty was convincing. At last
Annie, Sarah, Maggie, Joanna, David, Danny, and John
stood together at their father's bedside, seven of his eight
children.

John looked down at the old, lined face, so brown
against its circle of white hair. He noted the hands, restless with pain, and felt his heart flooded with pity. Once
Daniel had seemed the embodiment of power—dominating,
harsh, on fire with a sense of mission. Often he had been
cruel. Now he was a helpless old child, whose sands were
fast running out. His father—and he loved him.

He stooped lower, trying to reach the spirit that seemed
sleeping. Daniel's eyes opened; he looked up into John's
with a sudden awareness. "Is this my dear son?" he
whispered, then sank back into the old stupor. Later he
woke again and tried to pull John closer.

"My dear wanderer," he murmured, "My ain bairn."
A few hours later he was gone.

Another break came in the routine of John's days, this
time a fortunate one. Dewing and Company, publishers,
of San Francisco and New York, wrote to him about
a big, two-volume study to be called, "Picturesque California." Would he choose other writers and take the overall editorship? This offer was hard to resist. Louie, who

hated to see him so downhearted, urged him to accept.

"How can I manage the ranch and do the writing too?" John cried desperately.

"A way will open!" Louie answered.

John now tried to persuade first John Reid, Maggie's husband, then his brother Davie to come and manage the place for him, but both men refused. Even so, he started snatching what moments he could from the work of the ranch. At night Louie saw him bending over his work table, quill high in air, with an anxious look on his face. When he read snatches of it aloud to her, looking for a little encouragement, she was surprised to find how dull were his sentences, how uninspired his words. What had become of John Muir who wrote "The Humming Bird of the California Waterfalls," or the imaginative "Windstorm in the Forest of the Yuba"? Could she tell him? No, she must leave him to find his own way. It was not her fault, she knew; and yet he had come to the ranch and this humdrum way of life through her. She felt she could hardly bear it, if the John Muir she loved were to lose all his zest for life, all his creative fire. They belonged together, she told herself. Someway she must help him to open another door.

In summer, a year later, John and William Keith, who was to illustrate the new book, were off on a tour of the Pacific coast. John was far from well, yet writer and illustrator started out like eager schoolboys, tossing their burdens to the four winds. John thought that every mile of the region was etched on his mind and heart, but he needed to note the changes since his last visit and Keith could not sketch from memory.

When they reached the Shasta country, John was horrified at the new destruction wrought by axe and saw. "The glory is departing!" he cried bitterly. He decided then that his chapter on Shasta must be an attack on the ruin of the forests, a plea for a national park to save this region before it was too late.

Going on to Seattle and Puget Sound, he greeted, as if it were an old friend, the gleaming cone of Mt. Rainier high up in the heavens. He remembered how he had promised himself long ago, "Some day I'll return to climb it." He and Keith were joined by six other climbers and soon set out, via the Yellowjacket Trail. John forgot that he was ill and out of training. All the old urgency burned in his veins, the heady ambition to master that magnificent peak. Later he wrote to Louie, "Did not mean to climb it, but got excited and soon was on top."

Perhaps it was easier for Louie to write what she felt than to say it to John directly. On his return from Rainier, he found her letter waiting for him in his hotel mailbox.

The Alaska book and the Yosemite book, dear John, must be written and you need to be your own self, well and strong. . . . There is nothing that has a right to be considered beside this, except the welfare of our children.

As he read her understanding words, John felt that he had found hope and courage. Yes, together, they might be able to work things out! It was like a clear, cold mountain wind blowing in his face.

He came back from his trip full of ambition, ready for the future, only to be caught again in the desperate squeeze of more work than he could manage. He must go on with his book while the look and feel of things were fresh in his memory, but the needs of fruit growing had to be met at once.

When the tension was at its worst, John's only hope was to run away to a place where he could not see the ranch. A single room in a San Francisco hotel, where he could write all day long, where no one spoke to him— that was the solution.

In June, a year after the Rainier climb, another opportunity came to Muir, the most fateful of all. Robert Underwood Johnson, the editor who had always remembered and liked his sketches for the old *Scribner's*, was coming this way, looking for fresh, vivid material; something to increase the circulation of the *Century Magazine*, something to make jaded easterners sit up. How about a series on gold hunters of the old West? Would Muir contribute to it, come to see him, give him advice?

Not long after that, Johnson was standing in the doorway of his room at the Palace Hotel in San Francisco, first looking at his watch, then glancing down the corridor. He had wanted to meet Muir for a long time, but now he was annoyed. Didn't the man know he had other appointments? Why had he chosen to keep him waiting? Then he heard a distant shout, which seemed to roll on toward him. "Johnson, Johnson, where are you?"

He looked into twinkling blue-gray eyes, alive with humor, and heard a very Scotch voice saying, "My apologies, Johnson! I always do get lost in these confounded artificial canyons!" From their first laugh together the two men were friends.

Several days later Johnson was clinging to the seat of a rocking stagecoach, which was bowling along at the edge of dangerous cliffs, through clouds of dust, on the way to Yosemite. Muir beside him, using both hands freely, pointed out this tree or that, a Douglas fir three hundred and fifty feet high, or glacial marks on towering granite. They spent the night at Wawona. When Johnson was taken to the nearby Mariposa Grove, he became forever a captive to its beauty. "Incredible!" he cried. "One doesn't know trees till one has seen California!"

While Johnson rested, Muir wrote to Louie. "A glorious ride through the forests. Johnson was charming all the way. I mean to hire Indians or horses or something to make a trip to Big Tuolumne Meadows and Tuolumne Canyon. How much we'll be able to accomplish will depend on the snow, the legs, and the resolution of the *Century*."

There was nothing wrong with the resolution, John found, but the legs were another matter. They were used to city pavements, to being tucked quietly under an editor's desk. As the two men wandered about the Tuolumne country, poor Johnson stopped trying to keep up with Muir's easy lope. Once John looked back, to see him slip on a steep talus, covered with sliding stones, flounder, almost fall, trying frantically to save his glasses. John rescued him and found a place to rest. But he could not resist sly digs at "tenderfeet" and "taluses." Since Johnson took it in good part, this endeared him further.

One night as they camped beside Soda Springs, they sat late by their fire, watching the June moon rise slowly over the range, watching the tall peak of Unicorn and the towers of Cathedral etched black against a pale sky. Before them stretched the level plain of Tuolumne Meadow, dim, mysterious, caught in its amphitheater of mountains, ridden by phantom shapes of moonlit mist. Night noises fluttered from the forest; cold winds brought the scent of fir and pine.

"You say you see great changes here, as well as in the Yosemite?"

"Haven't you noticed the freshly charred stumps? The flowers are gone that should be here—ferns, even bushes, eaten. Young trees chewed to the ground. Soon only the rocks will be safe from the hordes of sheep, the terrible hoofed locusts!"

With rising passion Muir talked on and on, while Johnson, already under the spell of the Sierra, listened, deeply moved.

"Suppose we form a compact tonight, campfire agreement, what you will. You write down what you've just told me. Give me two articles. Then we'll work for a national park surrounding the Yosemite. I'll get a bill sponsored—take it to Washington."

"No use!" John cried bitterly. "Just eight years ago I worked on such a bill. The legislators scorned it. They killed it in committee."

"This bill won't die, I promise you," Johnson cried earnestly. "I'm used to lobbying—just spent weeks in Washington working for the new International Copyright law. But you must help me to rally support, rouse public opinion. You have the gift of words. Make them winged and barbed this time!"

"By Jove, I will!" John cried, then lapsed into silence. Was it the reflection of the firelight? As Johnson watched him, he thought he saw a radiance shining in Muir's face, a look of passion and dedication. A very John the Baptist, set in bronze by Donatello, he thought. And Muir felt that he had just been shown the way to a mountain peak which all his life he had meant to climb.

John came back from his trip to the Yosemite on fire with a new ambition; or rather, it was the old ambition burning with a brighter flame. Perhaps now all his years of wandering would be justified, crystallized into a set purpose. What seemed aimless might have been preparation; what seemed selfish could be turned to the public good. With all his knowledge, all his experience, all his influence, he would work toward one goal—to save from their exploiters the mountains and forests he loved.

He sent an article to the *San Francisco Bulletin*, which was glad to welcome him back. Other papers accepted letters and appeals. Though John knew the Valley itself could hardly be made a part of the newly planned national park, yet he pointed out abuses under the present California management. Eight men, shortsighted politicians, changing with every shifting governor, were running the Valley for the benefit of a "combine" that owned hotels and stables, plowed up meadows, and cut down trees to make hayfields for horses, mules, sheep, cows, and hogs.

If the national park were formed around and above the Valley, at least all the watershed forests could be saved. Without them, the Valley itself would become little more than a "charred stump."

John Muir's name still held the old magic. Nature lovers who had warmed to his earlier appeals came to his support now, men like Colby, Keith, William D. Arms, LeConte. Eastern papers quoted the letters. Here was John Muir again, the Alaska explorer, the man who had searched for De Long. This was news!

Vanished were the limping sentences which had worried Louie. The old eagle's quill seemed to leap into action almost of itself. "Barbed words"—yes. The good strong, simple, hard-hitting words of a propagandist.

By June two long articles were ready for the *Century*, and "Picturesque California" had been finished. But spring found John "shadowy" again. It was Louie's word for it, when she found him thin and tired. Also the bad cough had returned.

"I'm going to Alaska for a bit of wilderness health," John said to his doctor.

"The end of you, if you go."

"If I don't go, you mean," John answered firmly.

Soon he was on the steamer, *Queen*, heading for Sita-dakay, the bay where he had found the great glacier that was forever to bear his name. Now he started on a sled journey into solitudes no man had seen. He made the sled himself out of spruce boughs, pieces of lumber, and runners shod with steel strips. While young Loomis of the Rainier expedition camped at the lower moraine, he explored the upper reaches of the glacier—alone.

John returned in September, strong and well, to find that Johnson had been true to his promise. He had been lobbying hard for the new Park bill, which General Vendever had introduced to Congress. Would it die in the Lands Committee, as John's earlier bills had done?

The news was both good and bad. "Your articles," Johnson told him, "have roused the people. Telegrams, messages, are flooding Washington. Noble, Secretary of the Interior, is with us. President Harrison is on our side, but. . . ."

The "but" was a vicious smear campaign, which John Irish, California politician, member of the group which managed the Valley, had started against Muir. "Letters to editors and Congressmen, savage and vulgar; lies and yet more lies!" Johnson wrote in disgust. The first letter had been published in the *Oakland Tribune*.

"Mr. Muir cut and logged and sawed the trees of the Valley with as willing a hand as any lumberman. When the State became trustee of the grant, Muir and the mill were expelled. The State got there in time to save the forests from Mr. Muir."

For perhaps the first and the last time in his life, John published a statement in his own defense.

To the Editor of the Tribune:

I would state that twenty years ago I was hired by Mr. Hutchings to saw lumber from fallen timber. . . . I never cut down a single tree in the Yosemite, nor sawed a tree cut down by any other person. I never held any sort of claim in the Valley, or sold a foot of lumber. I would refer you to Galen Clark, guardian of the Valley.

John Muir

All through his years of work for conservation, Muir was to be the victim of cruel rumors, used to poison the minds of Washington. The interests, whose plans he worked to block, stopped at nothing. In time John managed to brush these from his mind as so many small, though vicious, gnats. Sometimes his wry sense of humor found them amusing.

The Yosemite National Park bill became law on October 1, 1890. United States Cavalry rode in to the new territory, to repel intruders and guard the land. Muir and Johnson and all the people who loyally aided them had won. In the same year, while Congress was still in favor of conservation, two other parks were established—

the Sequoia and the General Grant National Parks.

Now, at the end of October, John was about to start for the Kings River Valley of the South Fork to gather material for the *Century*. But soon he wrote to Johnson that the trip was given up, for Dr. Strenzel had just died.

His work was done and well done and closed like a summer's day, but it is sad to see the heartbreak of little Wanda and Helen. Night after night Helen wakes up and tells her mother, "My grandpa came to me and took me in his arms and kissed me. He is strong and carried me as he used to do. Why can't Grandpa come in the daytime?"

Soon the habits of the Muirs changed. They left the little white house they loved and joined Mrs. Strenzel in her big, pretentious Victorian mansion, elegant in its time, with the typical square-hat cupola of its day. John, who thought it ugly and disliked the move, had one compensation—a big study on the second floor where he could work in peace.

Carried forward on the government's wave of enthusiasm, Muir and Johnson now dared a measure to extend the boundaries of the new Sequoia Park. They wished to include the Kings River Canyon and two more magnificent stands of timber, but this time lobbying sheepmen and lumbermen were too quick for them. The bill was kept "buried in committee."

The President and his able Secretary of the Interior

retaliated. By a rider attached to another bill, an act was passed by Congress which gave Harrison the power to establish the *first forest reserves*—a vast area of thirteen million acres, rescued from private use. For fifteen years this special "enabling act" was a useful tool in the hands of conservationists.

From editors, nature groups, and individuals came a flood of grateful messages. The Boone and Crockett Club sent in a special resolution of thanks. It was a portent of the future that this letter was inspired, signed, and delivered by a rising young politician named Theodore Roosevelt.

John was hard pressed in these days, what he called "sinfully busy." Dr. Strenzel's estate to settle, all the care of two ranches, increasing demands for more and more copy for the *Century*, and always fresh work for the conservation fight. Johnson was a ruthless editor when it came to putting on the screws, and Muir, who wrote slowly, resented it. Also he was always supposed to furnish illustrations. Nor did he like the liberties taken with his sentences. What he wrote he wished left as he wrote it! Yet, to the end, the two men were friends.

One thing Muir had learned from their last failure— the enemies of conservation were well-organized. By this means they had won. John, who had always avoided groups, now set himself to form one, and so the Sierra Club was born.

It was a hot day in May 1892 when a small number of men met in the San Francisco office of Warren Olney, men like Joseph LeConte, the famous scientist, Cornelius

Bradley, William Arms. Electing Muir to the chair, they drew up a set of aims, broad enough to attract different kinds of people.

They were to "explore, enjoy and render accessible the mountain regions of the Pacific coast; to publish authentic information concerning them. Second, to enlist the support and co-operation of people and government in preserving the forests and other natural features of the Sierra Nevada Mountains."

Mountaineers, hikers, and nature lovers, young or old, editors and promoters, armchair enthusiasts and the growing number of good citizens willing to work for the protection of the land—all these were welcomed. The club mushroomed till it became a powerful influence in the long fight for conservation.

Muir was jubilant when he came home to his family that night to tell them the story of "what happened." At last he had support for the hard days ahead. He had waged a lonely fight for the wilderness. He had been derided and despised. Now he would stand alone no longer.

Almost immediately the Sierra Club went into action. Well-organized stockmen and lumbermen managed to introduce the Caminetti Bill in Washington, which was to cut away almost half of the new Yosemite National Park. The park had been Muir's and Johnson's first great victory; they were angry and desperate. The bill had passed the House. Now the Senate was to decide.

Cleveland was about to be president. Noble must yield to Hoke Smith, who was said to favor the ruinous bill.

"That savage liar" named Irish was already lobbying, when Muir wrote to Johnson, "I think Mr. Irish is in Washington and, though wicked, like the Devil he is smart and has great power in dark places. Do what you can to make the light shine on him!"

The Sierra Club appealed to Congress. Muir worked through personal interviews, telegrams to senators, letters in the press. Irish was no match for that seasoned old campaigner, Johnson of the *Century Magazine*. The bill was tabled for the present, but over and over, till 1894, it was to rear its ugly head. John learned then that a park, once formed, was never safe. It was always subject to attack, always in need of protection. Eternal vigilance was the price of victory.

Conservation fared both well and ill in the time of Cleveland. For John these were varied, exciting years. Encouraged by Louie, he worked out his long-hoped-for plan to see Europe with one of his favorite friends. Keith, the artist, went on ahead to New York and John followed him across the country. He found him being wined and dined by the artist world, not yet willing to sail. John himself was discovered by the *Century* and introduced to all the celebrities, from John Burroughs to Mark Twain.

"Burroughs had just made a speech, eaten a big dinner and had a headache. So he seemed tired and gave no sign of his fine qualities," John wrote to Louie. But later the two men became friends. Muir was taken on to Boston, Cambridge, and Concord, to Brookline, where Sargent, the Harvard head of the arboretum, lived. He dined with

Emerson's son and stood reverently at Walden Pond. The comment he made to Louie was completely in character. "Walden is only about one and a half or two miles from Concord—a mere saunter; how people should regard Thoreau as a hermit on account of his delightful stay here, I cannot guess!" To the man who had stayed alone for days in a Sierra blizzard or traced an unknown glacier, this seemed incredible.

Then Europe. Though the English Lake District, the fiords of Norway, the glaciers of the Alps, and the beauty of Lake Como charmed and delighted Muir, it was his return to Dunbar, Scotland, "my own old town," that gave him the greatest joy. He found friends and cousins proud to claim him; he tried to climb once more through the little bedroom dormer window, the site of his first scootcher—and failed.

Dear Wanda:

Last evening I took a walk along the shore on the rocks where I played when a boy. The waves made grand songs, the same old songs they sang to me in my childhood and the long, eventful years in America were forgotten.

John Muir came home again that fall of 1893 to celebrate a great event, the publication of "The Mountains of California"—his first book, though he was over fifty and had written all his life. Articles in magazines and newspapers, journals jammed with material from cover to cover, these hardly counted. This was a book. Everywhere it was widely praised, especially by the great botanists, Sargent of Harvard and Hooker of England. John called it his "little Alpine thing," and wrote Johnson that he had really worked hard, killing adjectives and adverbs by the score and cutting off *verys*, *intenses*, *gloriouses*, *ands*, and *buts*. He knew his own weakness.

"The Mountains of California" was a good brief for conservation; it gave nature lovers new hope. It also aroused the opposition. Land rackets were common, special pleading for timber and mining interests flourished. A new government policy was needed.

Twenty years before, in his first article on conservation in a Sacramento newspaper, John had advised a government study of all the country's forests. Now at last the plan was coming through. In an effort to avoid politicians, Hoke Smith asked the president of the National Academy of Sciences to select the group. He appointed Sargent, head of the Harvard arboretum, as leader, and General Abbot, Professor Brewer, Alexander Agassiz, Hague, and Gifford Pinchot as members. Muir, who refused to be a member, was made adviser. The men were to serve without pay.

Throughout the long, hot, and dusty summer, John traveled with the group. From the Black Hills of South Dakota, through the woods of Montana, Wyoming, Washington, Oregon, and on up and down the California coast. Breaking off for a brief Alaska trip in August, he returned to join the others in September. To John this was an exciting chance to help accomplish what should have been done long before, though there was not one of them who failed to realize theirs was a thankless task. The report might be tabled or destroyed; surely it would be derided and attacked.

Muir, like the others, grew deeply disturbed at what he found. The Northern Pacific Railroad, stretching throughout the West, had been subsidized by an enormous land grant, 120 miles wide. Not only had it laid waste its right of way, but had appropriated and destroyed vast stands of timber north and south. When they came to the Grand Canyon, they found mining started in the heart of it, and the forests being ruined around it.

In California, destruction was widespread. John wrote about the trip in his journal, telling of bad accommodations, dangerous driving, strange hours, all the homely details of land and people.

Sept. 6th. Lunched at Trinidad, a dull, dead lumber camp. . . . The redwood has all been cut hereabouts and is a desolate expanse of black stumps.

Sept. 7th. From Pepper Flat we took a stage for Ukiah and had a wild drive through woods, along precipices in the dark. Changed horses at midnight. One horse was "green," had only been hitched up twice. Reached Dyerville at 2:30 A.M.

The inconvenience of travel, long weeks given without pay, meant nothing to John, compared with resentment at what he saw. This was his beloved country. Ruthlessly, selfishly, wantonly, it was being destroyed. As he looked on hills stripped bare by mining, fires, illegal cutting, the deep, cumulative anger grew and grew in his heart.

"Wherever the white man goes, the groves vanish," he thought. Over and over these words seemed to beat at his brain, till later they became the theme of one of his greatest, most unforgettable appeals to the American people.

The trip of inspection ended. Sargent wrote his report and sent it to John "for ideas and inspiration." Its main recommendation was the "creation of thirteen new reservations, distributed among eight western states." The findings were submitted to President Cleveland.

To John's great, though temporary, joy, the President responded at once. On Washington's Birthday he issued a Presidential order, setting aside the thirteen new government reserves, amounting to over twenty-one million acres. A short-lived victory, for the fat was in the fire now. The henchmen of the Senate, yielding to the furious demands of Western stock, mining, and lumber interests, spent two days (one of them Sunday) trying to impeach the President.

Failing in this, they passed a rider, tacked on to another bill, annulling the new reserves. But Cleveland also had a weapon. He promised to veto the bill as it now stood. When Congress adjourned on March fourth, the matter was still unsettled.

"Ye gods!" Muir wrote in wrath to Johnson. "What's

to be done with the crazy Senate, voting on the Holy Sabbath for diabolical destruction of forests? The Western Senators are a bad lot, but we'll win at last!"

Cleveland retired. McKinley was President. In an early special session of Congress the forest reserves came up again; the edict barring their use was set aside for a year, except in California. Here Muir's influence held. There followed a rush to file claims, parcel out tracts, establish private ownership. Most of the conservationists gave up in despair. John's will to fight grew stronger.

Now the *Atlantic Monthly* joined the struggle. Walter Hines Page, editor, wrote to Sargent, asking who would be the best writer to rouse the public. "Only one man capable of it," Sargent answered. "His name is John Muir."

Muir's first article for the *Atlantic* appeared in August 1897, an able and angry challenge to a captive Congress, an appeal to the people.

The forests of America, however slighted by man, must have been a great delight to God, for they were the best he ever planted. . . .

After the Atlantic coast from Maine to Georgia had been mostly cleared and scorched into ruins, the overflowing multitude of bread and money seekers poured over the Alleghenies into the Middle West, spreading devastation ever wider and farther over the rich valley of the Mississippi and the vast, shadowy pine region about the Great Lakes.

Then still Westward the invading horde of destroyers, called settlers, made its fiery way—over the broad Rocky Mountains, felling and burning more fiercely than ever, until now it has reached the wild side of the Continent and entered the last of the great virgin forests on the shores of the Pacific.

Every other civilized nation in the world has been compelled to care for its forests and so must we, if waste and destruction are not to go on, leaving America as bare as Palestine or Spain.

Of all the magnificent forests around the Great Lakes, once the property of the United States, scarcely any belong to it now. . . . Only the forests of the West are significant in size and value and these, though still great, are fast vanishing.

Any fool can destroy trees. They cannot run away; and if they could, they would still be destroyed—chased and hunted down as long as fun or a dollar could be got out of their bark hides, branching horns, or magnificent bole backbones. . . . Through all the centuries since Christ's time, and long before that, God has cared for these trees, but He cannot save them from fools—only Uncle Sam can do that.

Seven months after the appearance of Muir's first *Atlantic* article (there were ten of them in all) the question of the forest reserves came up again. The Senate voted to abolish them altogether, but the House, responding to the will of the people, had another answer. The American public, now better informed and alert, made its wishes known. The forest reserves were saved.

It was May. John sat writing to editor Page of the *Atlantic*.

I start tomorrow on a two months' trip with Harriman's Alaska expedition. John Burroughs and a lot of good naturalists are going. I would not go, were it not to visit the only part of the coast I have not seen.

This has been a barren year. I lost half the winter in a confounded fight with sheep and cattlemen and politicians; in the other half I was benumbed by sickness in the family. In word-works I'm slow as a glacier. You'll get your papers some time, if I live long enough.

Harriman, the great railroad magnate of the Northern Pacific, gathered over a dozen distinguished scientists, giving them every facility, from laboratories to private equipment. One hundred and twenty-six people were on board the *George Elder* when she started north to explore the coast of Alaska, Bering Sea, and St. Lawrence Island. Muir was on the planning committee. Burroughs thought it "a miracle and a mercy" that "cold-storage Muir" didn't take them on to Wrangell Land.

John Muir and John Burroughs were really friends, but each acted like a prima donna, liking center stage. Muir was forever needling Burroughs about all the admiring females who tucked him in with steamer rugs, and Burroughs was heard to say acidly, "Ask Muir a question;

when he answers, you'll get the whole of the glacial theory thrown in!"

As for Edward Harriman, their host, though Muir was opposed to him on principal as a "power-grabber," in personal relations he found him friendly and sincere. Harriman, who admired Muir, was later to help him at a moment of crisis. It was fortunate for John that he joined the expedition.

The year 1900. The Spanish-American War had been fought and won. The sinking of the *Maine*, the brave charge up San Juan Hill, had passed into song and story. On a wave of enthusiasm McKinley was returned to the White House. This time there was a new and untried vice-president, but not a man untried in experience, courage, or wisdom. Though still young, he had held many and varied jobs. He had been assemblyman, rancher and writer, president of the Police Board of New York City, Assistant Secretary of the Navy, colonel of the First United States Volunteer Cavalry and, after the war, governor of New York State.

Descendant of an old and proud Dutch family, he was no henchman of privilege, but a fighter against selfish and illegal power. He spoke with the authentic voice of the people. Platt, the gentle boss of New York State, had found him hard to handle, so now he was eased into the vice-presidency, before he could succeed himself as governor. Hating and resenting it, but being willing to serve, he called it, "taking the veil."

This man was a child of fate. McKinley went to speak at the Pan-American Exposition in Buffalo on September 6th, 1901. The next day, unguarded at a great reception, he was shot by an assassin and thirteen days later died. On that same day his successor was rushed to the White House. The oath of office was taken. So Theodore Roosevelt became the twenty-sixth president of the United States.

It was said that the change of scepter at once brought a wave of fear to the ranks of big business; not so to nature lovers. They knew that, as a governor, Roosevelt had shown an interest in forest protection, even calling down to Albany forty tough mountain guides to advise him on what the Adirondacks needed. Rough Riders of the West, who followed him up San Juan Hill, policemen of the city beat, or guides from the mountains—with all of them he could speak a common language.

After the inauguration, Richard Watson Gilder, editor of the *Century*, Johnson's boss, had an interview with the President and wrote about it.

"I talked with Roosevelt for nearly five hours, the second day of his life in the White House. He rings true! He is a noble fellow. He has an excess of temperament, but a serviceable conscience as well." A serviceable conscience! The truth of this John Muir was to learn.

In May, two years after he had become president, Roosevelt was about to start for the West. John also was about to start on a tour through Europe with his friend, Charles Sargent, when the word came to him secretly from Johnson that Roosevelt wished to see him. He was both pleased and annoyed. The sailing date was set; Sargent would be furious—but. . . . Immediately John wrote to Sargent that sailing must be delayed. "An influential man from Washington wants to make a trip into the Sierra with me and I might be able to do some forest good."

Would Sargent agree, and if he wouldn't, what then? Should he give up a tour planned for months just because of a sudden royal summons? Then a letter came, an envelope with *The White House* printed upon it in gold.

"I write to you personally to express the hope that you will be able to take me through the Yosemite. I do not want anyone with me but you and I want to drop politics absolutely for four days and just be out in the open with you." This clinched the matter, as Sargent himself agreed.

It was the middle of May when the President's special train reached Raymond, to be met by Muir with two rangers, pack mules, and cooks. At Mariposa Grove they managed to evade the throng of politicians and slip away into the shadows of the forest. What sense of rest and relief came to Roosevelt, as he found himself alone with the tall, spare man, of the easy manner and humorous blue eyes! Alone, except for unobtrusive helpers in the background.

That night, after the campfire flared and died, they lay down in the darkening aisles of the great sequoias. As the President's eyes followed the giant trunks up to their dim, waving plumes, shadowy against a clear sky, he felt that here were the pillars of a mightier cathedral than the Middle Ages had ever devised. Out of the darkness came the cool song of the hermit thrush and at dawn the voice of the forest spoke again.

The next day they took the trail to Glacier Point, camping on the edge of the Canyon Wall, high above the Yosemite, with huge silver firs as their bodyguard. On the third and last night the floor of the open Valley was their bedroom, facing the tremendous mass of El Capitan, while the falls roared in the distance.

As they followed the trails or sat by a campfire in companionable talk, a sense of trust and comradeship grew between them. Here is no lonely fanatic, the President thought, but a keen, practical man, well informed about the needs of his country. This is no self-seeking politician, Muir told himself, but a great man, humbly trying to help the people.

From hunting in South Africa to the discovery of Alaska glaciers, many memories of adventure passed between them, and over and over they came back to the problems of land and forests. Yet, as they talked, Muir grew increasingly anxious. Was he himself saying anything convincing? Could he make the President realize that the forests must be saved *now*—or else lost forever?

Theodore Roosevelt returned to Washington, moved by Muir's sense of present danger, with his own love of the wilderness rekindled and heightened. Then, before long, conviction grew into action. When he came to the White House, the extent of the forest reserves was over forty-six million acres. By the spring of 1909 he had set aside more than one hundred and forty-eight million acres of additional national forests, three times as much as had Harrison, Cleveland, and McKinley combined.

During his last three years he proclaimed sixteen national monuments, including the Grand Canyon. It was Muir who suggested this might be made a monument; then later it became a national park. Under Roosevelt the number of national parks also doubled.

No policy of his roused deeper approval, or sharper hatred, than his fight for conservation, but his own courage and decision managed to hold the line. The people helped him by appeal, petition, and support. At last they gained a vision of the wrong being done by the destruction of the forests with their beauty and riches which they still could save. In this awakening of the people the eagle's quill played a major part. John Muir's enthusiasm and Roosevelt's serviceable conscience turned the tide.

13

Dauntless Soul

THOUGH DELAYED, MUIR AND SARGENT WERE SOON ON their way to Europe, visiting France, Finland, Russia, the Black Sea and the Caucasus, the Eastern Ukraine, Siberia, and part of Manchuria. Leaving Sargent at Shanghai, John called on the Harriman steamship agents to help him plan the rest of his trip.

Soon he was sailing along the coast of China, with India as his objective. The magnificence of the Himalayas moved him to "thank God he had been led to see them." Near Simla the deodars, "wonderful God-trees," reminded him of his own redwoods. The climax of his trip in Egypt was a voyage up the Nile.

Now he was homeward bound, via the Orient and the South Seas, about a three months' trip. Australia, the Philippines, then China again. On Christmas Day he grew increasingly anxious about his family. Too long away, he reproached himself in his homesickness. A strange fear that Helen was dangerously ill haunted him. He tried to brush this away as a phantom of loneliness, but still it followed him.

A cable from Harriman at Canton invited John to return on the steamship, *Siberia*. A little more than a year after he had left, on a beautiful day in May, he saw the coastal hills of California and sailed through the Golden Gate, knowing by the sudden sense of joy how hungry for home he had been.

As the little tug eased the steamer in, Wanda and Helen stood waving from the San Francisco dock, grown tall, handsome, wonderful to see! They, in turn, were delighted to find how strong and well their father looked. At the ranch, with John Reid and his sister Margaret, Louie was waiting.

When the first excitement and exchange of news was over, Louie told John quietly of Helen's hard fight with pneumonia, in the days when he had been lingering in Australia. He knew then that all his imaginings had not been phantoms. Harshly he turned on himself in an instant of self-reproach.

"You stayed to fight for her life, while I was amusing myself."

"You did not know," Louie answered gently.

John returned from his year's trip, wishing little more than to be reacquainted with his family, enjoy quiet days with Louie, or go hiking with Helen over the hills— Helen, who was always his eager comrade. But there was a harsher fate in store for him.

He had only himself to blame. His *Atlantic* articles had been republished in a book, called *Our National Parks.* It helped to rouse the people. His own brain child, the Sierra Club, was seething with ambitious plans. This was the time, they told him, to start a new fight for "recession," the term then used to describe giving land back to a former possessor. If the Yosemite were allowed to go back (or recede) into federal control, it could be made part of the big national park already established above and around it and would at last be well cared for. Surely they could count on his initiative and leadership? The governor of California was with them. The President was certain to respond.

"I think so," John answered cautiously. "Last year, when he was with me in the Valley, he was so moved by its grandeur that at first I thought he saw little else. Who but a blind man could feel differently? Later he agreed with me that the entire central section looked trampled and neglected, dusty and pathetic like an abandoned pasture. In the end, he noted charred stumps, chewed bushes, the absence of flowers and ferns."

By fall the fight was joined. Again the place Muir loved best of all was the object of a struggle between selfish interests and the men and women who wished to save it. Against recession were all those who stood to gain by their control of Yosemite, the eight so-called directors, who would lose their salaries; the railroad, stagecoach and hotel interests, with political grafters spawned by them. William Colby, secretary of the Sierra Club, drafted a bill at John's request. It was introduced in the state legislature. In Colby, Muir had a young, vigorous, and convinced helper, well-trained as a lawyer. It was part of Muir's genius that such men were willing to join him at a time of need. In Colby he had found one of the finest, a powerful ally.

Throughout California the press was vocal—and divided. Some newspapers lashed at the bill with frantic phrases.

"Those who vote for recession must be traitors. . . . State pride should prevail. . . . Yosemite is the state's big advertisement. Why give it away?"

The old whispering campaign started once more, against "John Muir, that ignorant sheepherder who cut down trees in the Valley." This time John met the gibes with silence.

Nine times the two men went to Sacramento to lobby, make speeches, deal with hostile politicians, appeal for the bill. It passed the assembly by 45 to 20, but the real fight would be in the senate. Staring failure in the face, Muir appealed to Harriman. The Railroad King, who remembered days of comradeship on the Alaska cruise, telegraphed his chief counsel in San Francisco to push the bill. Now the powerful railroad lobby was behind it; politicians changed sides over night—and recession won.

If John, in the midst of victory, felt a qualm of conscience, he did not show it. But he had no illusions. He knew that he had fought fire with fire. He had turned to one of the strongest of the interests to help defeat the rest. But the people, vocal with letters and telegrams, had played their part too.

John himself was exhausted. In spite of his best resolves, he had deserted his family for days at a time. As for poor Colby, he had had to be away when his first son was born. A friend of his, abetted by John, suggested that the baby be named "Recession Bill."

The struggle at Sacramento was only a miniature of the conflict to come. California had voted to cede the Valley back again to the nation. Would the national government accept it? In Washington the bill was held up for over a year, while stockmen and lumber companies tried again to chisel away part of the national park. Speaker Cannon delayed action "on grounds of economy."

If the bill were held up longer, the California decision would be "null and void." Desperate, John appealed again to Harriman. Speaker Cannon had a sudden change of heart. In both House and Senate recession won.

"Sound the timbrel! Let every Yosemite tree and stream rejoice!" was Muir's word to Johnson. "The fight we planned by that campfire seventeen years ago is at last fairly, gloriously won—every enemy down, derry down!"

All through these hard days of fighting, John was facing trouble at home. Helen had been attacked again by her old enemy, pneumonia. In his sympathy and anguish at her suffering, he felt that he was torn in two. "I can never get the sound of her coughing out of my ears," he wrote to a friend. Even when the worst seemed past and recovery certain, the doctor said that she must be taken to drier country. In May, with Wanda as his staunch helper, John took her south to the Arizona desert near Wilcox.

Louie, as always, elected to carry all the burdens of the home in their absence. If she grieved at the separation and dreaded to have a beloved child taken away from her care, there was no word or look of reproach, no sign of resentment in her clear, gray eyes. Yet in her own mind there must already have been fear that she might never see Helen again.

A month after they were settled in the South, a letter came from Louie. She had been ill, but they need not worry—she was better. Then it was only a matter of days before John was called home. Taking his daughters with him, he rushed back to Martinez. For a few days Helen stayed with her mother, then the doctor intervened. "That child must be hurried south at once," he told John. So an elderly friend was sent with her to Arizona.

For a little while longer Louie lingered, brave, indomitable to the end. On August sixth she died. To John, in the days that followed, life itself seemed unreal. The house that yesterday had been a center of warmth and happiness was now only a series of hollow, echoing rooms. He wandered through them—lost, ghostlike, destroyed.

How shallow he had been when he told her that there was no separation for those who loved each other! Death was the final separation. Death was a high wall, a closed door, an eternal silence. Now he regretted all the lovely days they had missed being together. He had been a spendthrift of time. This was his punishment.

But the bitterness passed. In the end, it was Helen's need that saved him. Taking Wanda, he went back to the desert. Like shapes on a screen the days passed. John managed to live them one by one.

"Get out among the mountains and the trees, dear friend, as soon as you can," Theodore Roosevelt wrote to him out of his deep understanding, but John could not go wandering now. As Helen grew better, they all took long rides over the desert country and John forgot himself in the joy of motion and the charm of this unfamiliar land. Soon his beloved Midge seemed really well, pneumonia forgotten and that still more dire threat of tuberculosis averted.

It was the April after Louie's death, and the three of them were still exploring the Arizona country, when news came of a tragedy, one of the worst disasters in American history. Early on the morning of April 18th, a terrible earthquake, followed by fire, swept the proud city of San Francisco into ruin, killing hundreds, leaving thousands homeless. Over four square miles destroyed. Only dynamite could stop the fire.

Martinez, almost thirty miles away, felt the deadly tremor. The lonely house of the Muirs, high on its knoll, bore its share. Well-built, with massive timbers and beams, it resisted the quake, but the great chimneys came tumbling down, plaster crumbled from inside walls, two of the mantels fell forward, spewing soot and rubble over the soft, old carpets.

The description of his home which reached John sounded deplorable, but he refused to go back. Gradually his zest for life was returning; he had made a new and fascinating discovery and Helen needed him. He sent back orders to have the worst of the damage repaired. The rest must wait.

One day, as he rode with Helen, they found a strange petrified forest, great stone logs of rainbow colors, lying in masses against the hot gold of the sand. Through incredible ages these trees must have completed their metamorphosis. The geologist in John was fascinated. Over and over he returned to study them. Later, in the University of California Library, he was to pore over every book he could find on fossilized forests. Then he would be ready.

He would appeal to President Roosevelt to save this strange and wonderful place from the railroad men, who were carting off huge logs to be chipped into tourists' souvenirs. If not a park, surely this could be made a national monument! John found a new interest, a new cause to battle for; life was good again!

In June Wanda went back to Martinez to be married to Thomas Rae Hanna, a civil engineer. They moved into the beautiful old adobe, only a quarter of a mile from the Muir home, but John, who had hoped that she would always live with him, found the distance too far. Later, when the "little mugginses" began to arrive, he was proud and happy over the marriage.

By August they were all reunited in Alhambra Valley. With grace and surprising maturity, Helen began to preside over the big house, aided by a young Japanese servant who adored her. Old Fong, the Chinese, was promoted to the care of bushes and flowers. Again in his big study on the second floor, with all the relics of his adventuring about him—the walrus tusks from Alaska, spears from Africa, the Indian basket filled with carved ivory toys—John turned painfully back to his writing. It had been so long—and Louie, his wise and kindly critic, was dead! Sensing his struggle, Helen taught herself typing and made up a kind of speed writing to help.

John began to look critically at his house. How dilapidated it looked! Now that it was a home again, with Helen its mistress, he must put everything in repair. Cleaning and painting first, the mantels replaced, then some structural changes. He ordered an arch cut between parlor and dining room, making a lovely vista where before they had been separate. New rugs and new draperies next —the best of everything from San Francisco shops. This was a place fit for his beloved Midge, and Dr. Strenzel would have approved!

That fall of 1907, Keith, his artist friend, lured John back to the mountains. The two men camped in beautiful Hetch Hetchy Valley, entrance to the Tuolumne Canyon and all the wild meadow land beyond. The falls at night, "like a ghost in the darkness," the magnificent reds, purples, yellows of the woods, the voices of the rushing stream, the timeless days, spoke to John with a new meaning. As with Christian in "Pilgrim's Progress," some terrible weight seemed to slip from his shoulders.

"Wonderful place!" Keith said, watching the campfire wood catch, flicker, then blaze, under John's expert hands. "Why do we go back?"

"Wish I knew!" Muir answered.

"As beautiful as Yosemite here."

"The cliffs are not so high."

"But the place has more charm. It would be a crime if it were ever spoiled."

There was a long silence, then Keith continued hesitantly, "I have heard rumors. . . . Is it true—that San Francisco has designs on it?"

"To dam the Hetch Hetchy, get free power, channel the water down? Yes."

Keith never forgot the flashing anger in John's eyes or the grim look of his tight-set mouth, but his words were controlled. "They can never win—never. Not as long as there is a breath to protest with, or pen to write." A month later, Muir had an article in the *Outlook Magazine*, "Tuolumne Yosemite In Danger."

John came back from the mountains that fall to another crisis. Helen had been coughing when he left; now she was struggling with a new attack of pneumonia. Again she rallied, but the doctor issued an ultimatum. She must go to Arizona and live there, at least for a number of years.

With all his hope of a happy home shattered, John took his daughter south and stayed to watch the building of a snug, comfortable little cabin, on the edge of the desert near Daggett. When he had found a good older nurse and companion, he returned to Martinez. Now he sent down to Midge everything he thought she might wish, her books and treasures, the dog Stickeen, named for the hero of Alaska days, her favorite horse, a big spirited animal called Art.

Over and over he gravitated to the South in these days, to visit Helen or to stay with other friends in Pasadena or Los Angeles. He was restless, eager for change, but he always returned to the lonely old house and the cluttered study and the silent devotion of his Chinaman, Fong.

Soon Helen was well again and married to Buel Funk, son of a desert cattle rancher.

In the summer of 1911 Muir's daemon of restlessness was riding him. How well he knew the familiar wanderlust! For the present the long-drawn-out Hetch Hetchy struggle was quiet. This was the time to go. At last he would sail down the Amazon, follow the dream of his youth, as Humboldt had.

When he told his friends, they tried to prevent his going. "South America for a man of your age?" "You'll catch malaria—or something worse." "You're not too well." John Burroughs said he had "gone gite, clean gite," but Muir answered with a hearty "Bosh." If his muscles were weaker, there was nothing wrong with his will power.

In New York he met his old ally, Johnson, and the two men went to Washington together. A speech on Hetch Hetchy to the famous Boone and Crockett Club, talks with Champ Clark, Joe Cannon, President Taft— at least he had done his farewell bit against the opposition!

For a few weeks he retired to a solitary cottage on Henry Fairfield Osborn's Hudson River estate. He was polishing two books, "The Yosemite" and "The Story of My Boyhood and Youth." Then, on August 11th, he took the steamer from New York.

From Pará, Brazil, he wrote back to his recent hostess, "Here at last is the River. Thanks to your loving care, I'm well and strong for all South American work. . . . Had a long, charming slide all the way to the equator between beautiful water and beautiful sky."

From Pará John sailed to Rio de Janeiro, from Rio on to Santos, and from there he struck inland, joining a party of lumbermen who were heading for the interior. He wandered for hundreds of miles, through millions of acres of ancient trees he had been so anxious to find, the *Araucaria Brasiliensis*.

Well, he thought, as he traveled on, studying the forests, now his life had come full circle. He was once more a wanderer, as in the days after college when he took his thousand-mile walk to the Gulf. He had written on his notebook then: John Muir, Earth Planet, Universe. That was still his address, wasn't it? Still a wanderer, answerable to no one except himself! But there was one difference. Then he had been free—but never lonely. He was still free, but now he knew loneliness too. What was Wanda doing? How was his beloved Midge? Would he ever find Louie again? This was old age. Yes, he had come full circle!

Then Buenos Aires. Here John was met by reporters, officials, local scientists, smothered with invitations and interviews.

"What are you going to write next?"

"Nothing until I give up my present job."

"What's that?"

"Tramp!" John answered lightly. "I'm 74 and still good at it."

For many years Muir had wanted to study another araucaria, the monkey puzzle, that strange, twisted pine which baffles even a monkey, so they say. He found them on the western slope of the Andes, a hundred miles from Victoria, and camped out for the night under their weird branches. Grotesques among trees—immeasurably old!

From Montevideo John sailed for Cape Town, South Africa, and took the train to Victoria Falls. Again he was looking for a little-known tree, the baobab, which he later said was like a hippopotamus. Though neither tourists nor hotel keepers seemed to have heard of them, a small Negro boy led him to a grove near the Big Falls.

Muir came back to America by way of the Mediterranean, reaching New York after seven months away. Everywhere in South America he had been welcomed and fêted. Though he did not know it, President Taft had sent word through the widespread consular service, asking them to watch for and give every courtesy to the traveler, John Muir.

John stopped in Hollywood, to which Helen had moved, and saw with pride the first little son, named for him. Then he went home to the ranch, happy in the welcome from Wanda and her three boys. Strent, John, and baby Richard came running and he flung wide his arms!

It seemed peaceful and right to come at last to the big house on the knoll, with its cypress hedge around it and the date palms at the turn of the driveway. There was the sequoia he had brought as a seedling from the forest and planted himself; here were Louie's beautiful cedars. He seemed almost to feel her beside him, as he wandered through the rooms, to climb at last to his own retreat.

The picture of live oaks by Keith, hanging over the mantel, the photographs and friendly backs of books, his own homemade wooden clock there in the closet—these made him welcome. They were his, his past around him, and this was right.

A moment of peace, as he sharpened his quill and started to outline a chapter or two for the new book which must be written. Something about Alaska. Should he call it simply "Travels"? There was so little time now. He must hurry on the work. 'Twould soon be dark! It was well that he had this moment of peace, for one of the great tragedies of his life was fast approaching.

* * *

Under two presidents the plan to dam the beautiful Hetch Hetchy Valley as a cheap water source for San Francisco was a political football, kicked and carried back and forth, but never making a goal. A serious obstacle was the constant shift of men in charge at Washington; no consistent policy could prevail. Roosevelt and Taft both left the White House. No decision was reached.

Then came Wilson. By a strange quirk of fate, he appointed as the new Secretary of the Interior the very lawyer who had represented San Francisco politicians, when the design on Hetch Hetchy was drawn.

Though discouraged, Muir and Colby rallied their forces. Johnson wrote editorials for the *Century* and *New York Times*. John placed articles, sent letters and telegrams, talked to friends. Out of his own pocket he met the expense for lobbying in Washington. Work on his book was dropped. He gave all his time, energy, and personal courage to the cause.

Leading newspapers across the nation denounced "the Hetch Hetchy steal." The American Alpine and Appalachian Clubs of the East worked side by side with the Mountaineers of the West, the Mazamas, the powerful Sierra Club.

Word went round that the so-called Raker bill, authorizing the seizure of the Hetch Hetchy Valley, would not be called out of committee until fall. But when most of the opposition were away on vacation and many congressmen absent, it was suddenly rushed through the House, with over two hundred members not voting. "Railroaded, meanly skulked and log-rolled through," as John said. If only he could turn to Harriman again! The Railroad King, with his far-flung empire, would help them. But Harriman was dead.

In November John wrote to Helen, "The Hetch Hetchy question will probably be decided in December. I still think we will win. Anyhow, I'll be relieved when it's settled, for it's killing me."

In December the Raker bill passed the Senate. President Wilson, knowing little about the problem and caring less, refused to veto it. The beautiful valley was doomed. To John the outcome of his long struggle was a terrible disappointment. He had won before; he had hoped, even expected, to win again. A lifetime of dedication seemed lost in this bitter failure.

At first he thought so, then later he saw more clearly. He saw that it was all part of a wider struggle between the people and selfish interests who were striving to build a monopoly of power and water sources. In other times and situations, in differing forms, this same struggle would return. Greed against "forest righteousness"—over and over through the years. The American people must learn to protect their own.

The letters he wrote to friends from his lonely, dusty study were heartbreaking, but they looked to the future.

To the Henry Fairfield Osborns he wrote, "Fortunately wrong cannot last, while *some compensating good* must surely follow."

To his staunch ally, Colby, he wrote, "Truth and

righteousness must prevail at last. Anyhow, we must be true to ourselves."

Even in defeat, disappointment, and old age, John Muir refused to despair.

The days wore on. John turned to his writing with Scotch doggedness. The book was growing, though he felt tired and ill. Again his old enemy, the cough, racked and tore him. Sometimes he thought that the thick autumn fog, which rolled up from the bay, was creeping into his brain. He had worked hard and been more stricken by the Hetch Hetchy failure than he knew. But "Travels in Alaska" must be finished.

Just before Christmas he was seized with a longing to see Helen and the boys. Saying good-by to Wanda, he left for the South. There was little in his satchel beside the manuscript of "Travels in Alaska."

It was bitter cold when he reached Daggett at two o'clock in the morning; after his automobile trip to the ranch he felt chilled to the bone. In the dry sunshine next day, cheered by the joyous excitement of the small fry, he felt better. But that night a wave of sickness seized him. Trying to rise from his big chair by the hearth, he fell. Helen, seeing the feverish flush on his cheeks, helped him anxiously to bed.

There was no hesitation on the part of the family doctor. "Pneumonia," he said at once. Helen's specialist in Los Angeles, summoned by telegraph, arrived early in the morning, bringing a nurse with him. Quickly he confirmed the verdict. "We must rush him straight to the hospital!"

And Helen, to whom the very word seemed like the crack of doom, began to make her father ready with loving tenderness. She packed his battered old satchel, then placed the carefully written sheets of his manuscript in on top. Then she reached for her coat.

"No," said the doctor, "let your husband come with us. You can't take little Johnny and you mustn't stop nursing him, now he is doing so well."

Heartbroken, Helen watched them drive away.

Stretched out in the hospital bed, John seemed peaceful—and better. The oxygen treatment eased him; fitfully he slept. The hours passed. It was a quiet moment when nurse and doctor were both out of the room. Suddenly a wave of coughing seized John with strangling grip. He tried to sit up, fell back on the pillow exhausted. Why was it growing dark in the room?

With fumbling fingers, he felt for the leaves of his manuscript, spread on the bed beside him. He raised one leaf, tried to bring it closer, but the page was a darkening blur. Was there someone beside him? "Louie?" he whispered.

There came a final struggle, a long, exhausted sigh. The sheet of paper, which he had clutched to the end, slid with a slow rustle to the floor. Alone, as he would have wished it, the brave spirit of John Muir went out on its final adventure, to meet the last and greatest mystery of all. When the nurse came back into the room, she was amazed at the look of triumph on his face.

They buried him beside his wife in the beautiful Alhambra Valley, near the old Strenzel pear orchard. It was the funeral of a conqueror, with a great throng standing reverently under the huge cedar tree and stretching into the distance, young and old, members of the Wisconsin Society and the Sierra Club, followers of the trails, friends from many cities, neighbors from nearby.

They lined his grave with sequoia branches and on his coffin they placed one great, sweeping plume. It lay there side by side with a laurel wreath of victory, tied with purple and gold, sent by the American Academy of Arts and Letters.

"I am the resurrection and the life, saith the Lord. Whosoever liveth and believeth in me, shall never die." The beautiful words drifted out to the silent throng. They were no travesty at the grave of John Muir, for he had always believed them.

"It seems easy to die, when great souls go before," he had written. "Blessed it is to feel that they have gone ahead to meet us, when our own day is done. The Scotch have a proverb 'The evening brings a' hame.'"

To John Muir, down through the years, there have been many tributes. At the unveiling of a bronze study of him by Pietro, President Charles Van Hise of the University of Wisconsin said: "Probably to Muir's leadership, more than that of any other person, is due the adoption of the policy of national parks. . . . Mingled with love, came ardent admiration for his tall, sinewy frame and

almost worship for the inner fire, which burned on his strong and noble face."

Enos Mills, one of Muir's great contemporaries, said: "The grandest character in national park history and nature literature is John Muir. His memory is destined to be forever . . . with every song that Nature sings in the wild gardens of the world."

Theodore Roosevelt, at Muir's death, said simply: "His was a dauntless soul."

Muir had received honorary degrees from four universities—Harvard, Yale, the University of Wisconsin, the University of California.

Throughout the country there are many memorials to him. In Wisconsin there is the recently created John Muir Park, on the site of his first boyhood farm. Fountain Lake and the meadow he dreamed of saving, "as a piece of pure wildness," are part of it.

In Madison, behind old North Hall, there is Muir Knoll, with a boulder on its top. Here John stood and looked back for a last, farewell glimpse of his beloved university before he wandered on.

In the Yosemite there is the John Muir Trail. Beginning in the north at Yosemite Valley, it extends south to Mt. Whitney, keeping as close as possible to the crest of the "Range of Light."

In Alaska there is the great Muir Glacier in the place now called Glacier Bay, Sitadakay by the Indians, a mountain of ice which John discovered and explored alone.

But best loved and appreciated by Muir himself was

the national monument presented in his name by the Honorable William Kent of Marin County, California. Muir called it "an encouragement to God." At the end of the Golden Gate Bridge, that touches Marin County and leads the wayfarer on to wild, rugged Mt. Tamalpais, there lies a stretch of forest called Muir Woods. Perhaps no man ever had a more fitting memorial.

Here, in all their original beauty, untouched by ruthless greed, the redwoods stretch their tremendous length toward the sky. So beautiful, dim, and lonely the place, so massive the great trees, the passer-by stands hushed and silent, as if in a place of worship not made by man. He feels, if he can put it into words, that he is back at the dawn of creation and that out from the shadows some huge, prehistoric beast may presently glide.

Muir Woods—a fitting monument to the man who could not stand idly by while selfish lumber interests were dynamiting and destroying for all time the oldest and greatest living things in the world.

Yet the most important memorials to John Muir are the national parks which lie in every part of our country —and in the people who come to them. Men and women, boys and girls, who may not even know Muir's name, find the joy of the long trail, the difficult climb, of nights under the stars. They will never forget their heritage; it becomes part of them. If need be they will fight to save it, so that their children's children may know it too—all the unspoiled beauty "in the wild gardens of the world."

Partial
Bibliography

Adams, Ansel and Newhall, Nancy. *This Is the American Earth.* Sierra Club Publication, 1960.

Atlantic Monthly. August, 1894.

Badè, William F. *The Life and Letters of John Muir.* Houghton Mifflin Co., 1923.

Colby, William E. "The Latest Evidence Bearing on the Creation of Yosemite Valley," *Yosemite Nature Notes*, Vol. XXXV, No. 1. Jan. 1956.

Cutright, Paul R. *Theodore Roosevelt the Naturalist.* Harper & Brothers, 1956.

Douglas, William O. *My Wilderness, the Pacific West.* Doubleday & Co., Inc., 1960.

Ellsberg, Edward. *Hell on Ice.* Dodd, Mead & Co., 1938.

Foerster, Norman. *Nature in American Literature.*

Gilder, Richard Watson. *Letters.* Houghton Mifflin Co., 1916.

Hadley, Edith J. *John Muir's Views of Nature and Their Consequences.* (Manuscript.) Ph.D. Thesis at the University of Wisconsin, 1956.

Johnson, Robert Underwood. *Remembered Yesterdays.* Little, Brown & Co., 1925.

Muir, John. "John of the Mountains," *The Unpublished Journals of John Muir*, edited by Linnie Marsh Wolfe, Houghton Mifflin Co., 1938.

——— *The Mountains of California.* Century Co., 1894.

Muir, John. *My First Summer in the Sierra*. Houghton Mifflin Co., 1911.

——— *Our National Parks*. Houghton Mifflin Co., 1901.

——— Privately printed correspondence with Mrs. Ezra Carr. Yale University Library.

——— *Stickeen, the Story of a Dog*. Houghton Mifflin Co., 1909.

——— *The Story of My Boyhood and Youth*. Houghton Mifflin Co., 1913.

——— *Travels in Alaska*. Houghton Mifflin Co., 1915.

Olson, Sigurd F. *Listening Point*. Alfred A. Knopf, 1958.

Osborn, Henry Fairfield. *Impressions of the Great Naturalists*.

Roosevelt, Theodore. *Autobiography*. Charles Scribner's Sons, 1906.

Shankland, Robert. *Steve Mather of the National Parks*. Alfred A. Knopf, 1954.

Sierra Club Bulletin. No. XIII

Teale, Edwin Way (Editor). *The Wilderness World of John Muir*. Houghton Mifflin Co., 1954.

Thwaites, Reuben G. *The Story of Wisconsin*. Lathrop Publishing Co., 1899.

Tilden, Freeman. *The National Parks*. Alfred A. Knopf, 1951.

Vroman, Charles. Unpublished Recollections of John Muir by his college roommate. University of Wisconsin Library.

Wolfe, Linnie Marsh. *Son of the Wilderness*. Alfred A. Knopf, 1945.

Yosemite Nature Notes. Vol. VI, No. 9, Sept., 1927; Vol. IX, No. 2, Feb. 1930; Vol. XV, No. 5, May, 1936; Vol. XVII No. 4, The John Muir Number, the Hundredth Anniversary of His Birth, April, 1938; Vol. XXXIV No. 11, Nov., 1955; Vol. XXXV, No. 10, Oct., 1956.

Young, S. Hall. *Alaska Days with John Muir*. Fleming H. Revell, 1915.

Acknowledgments

I wish to express my warmest thanks to the following publishers and libraries.

To Houghton Mifflin Company for the use of facts, incidents, and quotations from the books of John Muir, as well as from *The Life and Letters* by William F. Badè; and for the use of selections from *John of the Mountains, The Unpublished Journals of John Muir*, edited by Linnie Marsh Wolfe; also for the right to quote a statement about President Theodore Roosevelt from *The Letters of Richard Watson Gilder*, edited by Rosamond Gilder.

To Alfred A. Knopf for the use of material from *Son of the Wilderness*, a Biography of John Muir by Linnie Marsh Wolfe; for the right to quote a paragraph from *Listening Point* by Sigurd F. Olson, President of the National Parks Association.

To Fleming H. Revell Inc. for the use of material from *Alaska Days with John Muir* by S. Hall Young. The dialogue in the "climbing of Glenora Peak" is taken verbatim from Mr. Young's own reporting.

To Appleton-Century-Crofts, Inc. for the right to use three episodes developed in *The Mountains of California* by John Muir —his first discovery of a living glacier in the Sierra, the climbing of Mt. Ritter, the "windstorm in the forests of the Yuba."

To the Bancroft Library of the University of California in

Berkeley, California, for the use of manuscript material found in their archives—excerpts from the "Diary of Mrs. Strenzel," mother-in-law of John Muir; a letter from Muir to Professor James D. Butler of Madison, Wisconsin; selections from letters written by Muir to Robert Underwood Johnson, editor of the *Century Magazine*. Mrs. Muir also authorized this permission.

To the State Historical Society of Wisconsin for the right to quote part of a letter from "The John Muir Papers," written by Muir to Mrs. John Pelton of Prairie-du-Chien.

To the Memorial Library of the University of Wisconsin for permission to use part of an address delivered by President Charles R. Van Hise upon the occasion of the unveiling of a bronze bust of John Muir by the sculptor, C. S. Pietro, on December 6, 1916.

To the Yale University Library for the right to quote a critical note, written in Muir's own handwriting on the margin of his copy of Emerson.

To William E. Colby for excerpts from his article, "The Latest Evidence Bearing on the Creation of the Valley" in Vol. XXXV, no. I, Jan. 1956 of *Yosemite Nature Notes*.

Among many others, I owe special thanks to the following individuals:

To Mrs. Helen Muir, daughter of John Muir; to Mr. William E. Colby; to Mrs. Jean de Lipkau and Mr. Strenzel Hanna, grandchildren of John Muir; to Mrs. Strenzel Hanna; to Mr. Frank Swett and Mr. Westwood Wallace, co-ordinator of the John Muir Association; to Professor Andrew W. Hopkins of Madison, Wis.; Dr. Ernest F. Bean, former state geologist of Wisconsin; Dr. and Mrs. Alfred W. Swan of Madison, Wis.; Mrs. James Muilenburg of New York City; to the late Dr. Stanley A. Hunter and Mrs. Hunter of Berkeley, Calif.; to Mrs. Elizabeth Burroughs Kelley for permission to quote from her grandfather, John Burroughs.

To Miss Ruth I. Glass, librarian of the research library of the Yosemite Museum; to Mr. Douglas H. Hubbard, Park Naturalist; to Mr. Baird Buckham, ranger at the Crane Flat station; to Miss Adelaide E. Steffen and Miss Louise Henning, research librarians at the Memorial Library of the University of Wisconsin; to Miss Josephine L. Harper and Mr. Paul Vanderbilt of the State Historical Society of Wisconsin; to Mrs. Julia McLeod, curator of manuscripts at the Bancroft Library of the University of California.